Featherstitch

FEATHERSTITCH

(A Filipino Immigrant's True Story)

MERIAM BANIEL DELA CRUZ

Featherstitch (A Filipino Immigrant's True Story)

Published by Wheatmark®
610 East Delano Street, Suite 104
Tucson, Arizona 85705 U.S.A.
www.wheatmark.com

Publisher's Cataloging-In-Publication Data
(Prepared by The Donohue Group, Inc.)

Dela Cruz, Meriam Baniel.
  Featherstitch : (a Filipino immigrant's true story) / Meriam Baniel Dela Cruz.

  p. ; cm.

  ISBN: 1-58736-614-2 (alk. paper)

1. Dela Cruz, Meriam Baniel. 2. Filipino Americans—California—San Francisco—Biography. 3. Immigrants—California—San Francisco—Biography. 4. California—Biography. I. Title.

E184.F4 D45 2006
973/.04959/9 2006921379

International Standard Book Number: 1-58736-614-2
Library of Congress Control Number: 2006921379

Contents

My Appreciation and Thanks to the Following
for Helping Me Make This Book a Reality

Our Lord Jesus Christ, Mama Mary, and the Holy Spirit
who made use of my nothingness to be their instrument in
writing this book for God's greater glory.

My parents, Porfirio, Sr and Monserrat Baniel, who
inculcated in us the importance of Christian moral values
and academic excellence.

My husband, Rodante and children, Jose Arnaldo,
Mae Charisse and John Albert for their understanding and
unwavering support of everything I do.

My brother, Porfirio, Jr. and sisters Madelene, Minviluz,
Minerva and Majella for being there for me always.

Eloisa Ticar for helping me start my labyrinthine walk

Dolores Matutino, who got my journalistic juices flowing to write this book.

Nancy Defensor for her technical advice concerning the inception of this book.

Ed and Mae Lourdes Combong, my spiritual alter-egos.

Ismael Firmalino, Jr., my legal consultant.

Ermin Baniel Nacor, my nephew, for his information technology expertise.

Robert D'Imperio, my brother-in-law who is a professional artist, for "feeling" my manuscript to eventually visualize its appropriate cover design.

Ron Damele and Louise Giusto for making my stay with their mom, Silvia, memorable.

Virginia Blach of Menlo Park for showing me how strong faith in the Almighty and an altruistic way of life are more important than material legacies.

Sister Miriam Walsh, MSHS, Director of the Pastoral Department of the Laguna Honda Hospital in San Francisco, Ca. and my co-volunteers in this institution:

Fr. Te Van Nguyen (Chaplain), Emilia Aloba, Art Calma,

Daniel and Marina Cayetano, Mary Casserly, Anne Duffy, Mina Emma, Maureen Fitzpatrick, Alan Fisk, Mary Hanley, Elaine Jones, Raphael Lahoz, Cora Leaño, Patrick and Bea Malloy, Herminia Otstott, Ted and Jeanine de Riviera, Pura Rodriguez, Jerry Rough, John Scott, Nancy Sewell, Barbara Squibb, Eldina Tronco, Vicky Umale and Judy deVera – may your tribe increase!

Sisters of the Missionaries of Charity in San Francisco, Ca. and Tayuman, Manila, Philippines for exposing me to the teachings of Mother Teresa of Calcutta.
Knights and Ladies of the Miraculous Medal at the St. Vincent de Paul Parish in Manila, Philippines:

Reverend Mario Castillo, C.M., Apricacion Alindogan, Edgardo and Lucy Diaz, Imelda Fornea, Victorino and Lita Jalandoni, Esperanza Malong, Angelita Muñoz, Francis and Helen Tan.

Last but not least, to my production editor, Susan Wenger, for her constructive suggestions and insights relevant to publishing my first book here in the U.S.A.

Introduction

"FEATHERSTITCH" taken as a noun is defined by the *American Heritage Dictionary*, 3rd edition, as an "embroidery stitch that produces a decorative zigzag line."

When I was mulling over the appropriate title of my memoir, I thought I wanted one which though suggesting a rather light mood is symbolic of my life's experiences for the first five years in the US - colorful and rich yet with its ups and downs just like in a featherstitch with the stitches not on a straight line horizontally but follow a zigzagging pattern of going up until it reaches the climax and then down to gather momentum before it goes up again.

Anybody could write his autobiography with a purpose or several purposes in mind. Mine is to present to my readers real-life situations to entertain them; to "tease" their imagination which I hope will not go to the extent of giving them "mental indigestion"; and to bring them to a new level of awareness when what they thought of as unthinkable before is there existing in the status quo - but with a moral lesson behind which is the least common denominator of all these. Undeniably, how they are going to react to this last trend of thought is beyond my sphere of influence.

I am aware that no two people could have the same perception and rationalization of a given scenario so that I do not expect all my readers to share my views. Subjectivity cannot be considered a form of human weakness where an honest self-expression is concerned. Nor can it be alleged to be a camouflage for a hidden agendum with a selfish end as its objective. Likewise, discerning for spiritual meaning in every episode is misconstrued as an escape hatch of a restless soul.

I opine that it is not a question of who has the better perspective but rather a respect for the difference in looking at things as presented to us. Perhaps, we could even learn from each other in this way and broaden our horizon in the process. A complementary relationship?

Some of the names of my characters have been changed to protect their privacy; ditto with some of the settings to guarantee of no constraints in any form that might be a possible consequence. But the plots, presenting the moral lessons that are the very purpose why this book is written, are "what is, is and what is not, is not; but not what is, is not nor what is not, is". In short, what happened is as it really happened.

Furthermore, I salute my characters in their "search for a greener pasture" in the "land of Uncle Sam." Though mostly of Filipino descent, they could be identified with any ethnic group who also have to lose their self-identity by choice because of the necessity to partake a piece of the American pie in the interest of the common good. They sometimes found themselves exploited and subjected to some form of human degradation leaving them no other alternative but to hang on to any stratagem in their desperate desire to legally start life and survive in their adopted country, their sad smile and nonchalant attitude just a charade for their callousness to life's bitter struggle, their acceptance of the inevitable and being pragmatic in making the most of it just to reach their goal.

Lastly, I consider it a great blessing to have been exposed to a lot of stark realities within the American context, both personally and vicariously. The cultural differences that gave me an initial shock; the diversity and complexity of the personalities I had met and interacted with; the web of situations I was entangled in that led me to do some soul-searching apropos the relevance of my emotional, intellectual, and moral convictions based on the values I was brought up to the American scenario: all these enabled me to grow and mature as a person. It eventually led me to the conclusion that given the trials, question of choices and spiritual discernment in every action taken, getting started the hard way in a foreign land could still be colorful and rich though with its ups and downs just like the decorative zig-zagging design of a featherstitch.

I

Starting to Walk the Labyrinth

It was with a heavy heart April 1997 when I slung my bulging purse over my shoulder and followed my husband, Rudy, towards the waiting taxi. After checking that my suitcase and box filled with "pasalubong" (Filipino parlance for "gifts") were safely tucked at the baggage compartment of the cab, he sat down beside the driver and instructed him to drive towards the Ninoy Aquino International Airport, where I was supposed to embark on my second trip to the US. With my daughter, MC (short for Mae Charisse) three months short of her sixteenth birthday beside me, I tried to hold back my tears when I looked back for the last time towards my other two kids, Arnold (short for Jose Arnaldo) and Albert (short for John Albert), then 17 and 13 respectively, waving good-bye to us from our rented house at Metrica Street, a narrow road in the center of Manila.

Rudy and I had agreed earlier not to bring any of our kids to the airport and this we still had in mind after dropping off MC at our restaurant, a five-table eatery we had been operating for the past twelve years at San Marcelino Street, also in Manila. It was one of the five two-level commercial units that we found it hard to make both ends meet despite our legitimate business strategy to run a boarding house for students and middle-class working people on the second floor and a small eatery or grocery store or any other income-generating project on the ground.

In the Philippines, a small business like ours runs this way: with a few bucks saved coupled with some loans from your relatives or friends, you buy the "right" to occupy, renovate, and operate a business venture. In most cases, the owner of the building does not even know about the "arrangement" between the old and new tenants but if he does, he does not care a bit as long as the new operator of the unit pays the rent (which increases every year) regularly on a monthly basis subject to the penalty for late payments and maintains the wear-and-tear of the place. This is not to mention the license to operate, electricity, water, gas, manpower, and other incidental expenses that are the other causes of the operator's migraine so much so that whatever "profit" there is after deducting his overhead from his gross income is simply enough to maintain his sanity.

"Please take care of yourself and our kids," I sadly told my husband as we kissed each other good-bye at the pre-departure area of the airport. During our entire eighteen years of marriage, we were not so much keen on verbalizing our "I love you" towards each other (specially with me who is not the demonstrative type), although he still gives me flowers or gifts on special occasions, a carry over of his courtship, which started at the YMCA tennis courts, also in Manila, where we met and became partners on mixed doubles matches and later on, our engagement days, when he pampered me, treating me like I was a princess, which should be considering he is nine years my senior.

Rudy and I believed that marriage could be made more substantial by doing and maintaining the vow we made before God on our wedding day June 9, 1979, rather than simply saying it and forgetting about it afterwards when already entangled in the web of the daily activities. Physical distance may make the heart either forgetful or fonder, as they say, but as two adults and aware of the true meaning of our commitment towards each other and our children, we are sure somewhere, somehow, we could still get connected on the emotional and spiritual levels.

II

In Introspection

Sitting in the waiting lounge of the pre-departure area of the airport, I was in a hodgepodge mentally as I reviewed the months preceding my trip. My decision to go back to the US was not made overnight by Rudy and me. Unlike my first trip in 1995, this time the "why" behind my action was more than a pleasure trip. A financial break was now foremost in my hierarchy of needs. After much prayer for the right decision with the help of my mentor in our prayer group, Dr. Sinforosa Yasa, who is herself an intellectual giant in the spiritual microcosm, I discerned that God wanted me to go back (I always base my decision from trends). Otherwise, He should have improved our finances in the domestic front. Our restaurant business was not doing fine and my salary as English professor at a local Catholic university in Manila was so low that even my having gotten an "Excellent" rating during our students' teacher behavior inventory and my Mass Communication students having shed tears during our last day of classes could not make me change my mind. It is true money may not be everything but it is necessary. Also, life being a series of trade-offs, I realized Rudy and I could not afford to give our three kids that quality of life we wanted to if I'd just stay put, so inevitably one of us had to move. Sentimentalism sometimes has to give way in realizing the stark realities of life, which spark that altruistic desire to do something to improve one's lot for the common good, that "nagging bug" that drives our Filipino overseas contract workers, our country's unsung heroes, to look for greener pastures in the oil-rich Middle East like Saudi Arabia, Kuwait, and Israel; European countries like Italy and Great Britain; and nearby neighbors like Singapore, Korea, and Japan, leaving behind their month-old babies and older children still in the care of their extended family members. Another cost of this setup is the breaking up of some families where the spouse left behind, because of biological need, goes philandering or one's kids resort to drugs in the absence of parental supervision. Not to mention the ordeals the overseas contract workers (OCW's) might have undergone before leaving for their uncertain destination, when they were at the mercy of loan sharks or had to sell their only property, perhaps may just be a parcel of land inherited from their forefathers so as to pay their recruitment agencies, which sometimes they discovered to be operating rather illegally, duping them in the process.

Yet there are some "rags-to-riches" stories, too, just like when you see a jeepney (the common means of transportation in the Philippines) sporting a flashy billboard of "Katas ng Saudi Arabia" or "Juice of Saudi Arabia" or a neighbor's house built from the money sent by a daughter working as a nurse in London and a booming business enterprise from the sweat of a factory worker's brow in South Korea.

In my case, I rationalized that my husband loves our kids so much (all throughout their life, he has never laid a hand on them although he disciplines them verbally unlike I do, who believe in "spare the rod and spoil the child" aphorism), he can sacrifice to be a single parent to them on a closer context while I can do long distance parenting. Marriage for us means working as a team to achieve the desired objective even to the point of sublimating our conjugal needs. Our kids understood the rationale of my action and were all for it.

Another motivating factor was possible relocation for my family and myself in the "land of Uncle Sam" before the priority date of my sister's petition for us filed and approved in 1986 becomes current. I believe that one should keep her options open. If Plan A flops, then resort to Plan B; if Plan B fails, then go to Plan C; and so forth. There should always be contingency plans to fall back on. Furthermore, I am for the idea that if things happened beyond one's control, then there must have been a reason for such. As what we had learned in our philosophy class in college, for every effect there is always a cause although for every cause there is always no effect because there might have been an interference of action along the way that prevented the achievement of the desired objective.

This was not to mention the call I received from Dr. Domini, a respected podiatrist in Sunnyvale, CA, who was my former boss, a week before my scheduled flight to the US. He requested me to come over to be with his 90-year-old mother, Rose, who would be spending her vacation again with him in a couple of days. She was the lady I kept company with for five months the first time I was in the US from 1995-96. I had to admit that those were memorable days for me because it exposed me to the American culture. It gave me an initial shock but later accepted it as different from the culture I was brought up. I learned that children's addressing their grandparents or parents-in-law on a first-name basis (which we never do in the Phil), does not imply they have less respect for their older relatives; for it is just how they do things there. Or, where the parents of the bride pay for the wedding bills, that I had to assure Dr. Domini my father did not go bankrupt when he married us off, all five girls of us, because in our country, it is the honor of the groom and his family to pick up the wedding check. And how shocked he was (I almost split my seams laughing at his facial expression) when I told him how in the old days, the prospective groom had to even serve in the house of his "Galatea" (that sculptural work of Pygmalion who he later on fell in love with) doing all the domestic chores without any salary whatsoever at least a year before their actual wedding. When he asked me one time if we have women's liberation movement in the Philippines, I told him we don't need it because we women there are already the privileged gender without us asserting it. Why, even in the domestic front, *I* added, it is Dad who makes the decision all right but Mom has the final say or if ever it is Dad who has the final say, it better be not anything other than, "Yes, dear." Otherwise, he knows he is headed for trouble, knowing who has the upper hand. I also pointed out to him that here in the US, it is the girl who drives the boy home after a date as a favor for him. In our country, it is the other way around and isn't it flattering to us ladies? Or, when "pa-ME-la" is "PA-me-la" here in the US.

I was jolted from my reverie when a melodious all-male singing group broke the rather monotonous atmosphere that pervaded the pre-departure area. They rendered a beautiful well-blended song a capella that elicited a propitious round of applause from all of us afterwards. That was just cool.

"Ladies and gentlemen, you have just heard the 'Kundi-rana Group' from La Salle-Manila, who will begin a series of concerts in the Bay Area. We hope you like the song they had just performed for you," said the only lady in the group who, I presumed, was their adviser. I had been so deep in my thoughts a while ago I did not notice the group arrange themselves in three lines on one side of the lounge.Then, out of the corner of my eye, I saw the beautiful image of the "Lady of Good Voyage," about three feet tall dressed in green regalia on top of one of the chairs fronting the group as if she was the most honored guest which she really was.

Later on, when we actually boarded our plane after a nine-hour delay, the prayer I had privately muttered to myself a few minutes ago was answered when there on one of the seats at the first class section was the "Lady." Oh, boy, she will actually be with us on our flight to the US.

I was so happy I could cry!

III

Arriving In San Francisco

It was an early quiet evening when our plane touched down at the San Francisco International Airport. Unlike last 1995 when I first set foot in the US, this time I did not see the uniformed police officer in blue with his sniffing German shepherd who greeted us on one side of the stairs leading us down to the carousel where we picked up our luggage. Then, we had to queue, the tourists separately from the immigrants for our interview with the immigration officers who asked us the usual questions as to the purpose of our trip to the US: how long did we plan to visit and the like before stamping our passports indicating the date of our arrival and the allowable period of time we could stay here. This was followed by a visual inspection of our luggage which we had to open to be searched meticulously by the gloved personnel.

"Excuse me, but where could I line up to have my things inspected?" I asked a heavy-set uniformed guy in blue who happened to be idling nearby. I had seen two long lines of my co-passengers a while ago patiently waiting for their turn (I hated to wait, part of my nature, I guess).

He made eyeball-to-eyeball contact with me (I did not flinch a bit although he was 6'1" to my 5'1" stature), then looked down at my suitcase and the box of "pasalubong" for my parents and sisters who I knew were waiting for me outside, and then told me gruffly, "Over there," pointing to the "EXIT" sign..

Nobody stopped me from enjoying my nice walk in going out. Sometimes, looking like a country bumpkin can have its advantage. Right?

Or was it the "Lady" again calling the shots because she was right there tucked inside my suitcase in her image as the "Lady of Carmel," a souvenir given to me by Rodel, a one-eyed inmate inside the medium security camp of the national penitentiary in the Philippines, the venue of my prison ministry for the past five years where I had learned that a person is basically good. Circumstances sometimes make him otherwise, and not all those incarcerated are as guilty as we think they are, no matter how heinous the crime they had committed as defined in the penal code.

I had intended to give the image to my mother, who is also a Marian devotee.

It was a happy reunion that night with my parents, two sisters, and their families, whom I had not seen for a year.

I called up Dr. Domini after dinner informing him of my arrival and told him one of my sisters would drive me to Sunnyvale the next day, where he could meet me to bring me to his new house outside of the city. Rose, his mom, who had arrived two days before, was waiting for me. It was an understanding between Dr. Domini and his sister from Anaheim that Rose stays with the former for four months every year while the latter takes a break before resuming care of their mom for the next eight months. While at Sunnyvale, Dr. Domini wanted me to keep his mom company as her caregiver for $1,500 a month with two days off every week, free food, and lodging.

At this point, I would like to emphasize that "caregiver" here in the US, I found out, is one job title that most people find "unglamorous" and look down on because it means for them just taking care of the personal needs of an elderly or handicapped person; doing light housekeeping for him; being his nurse, secretary, driver, confidante - in short, being the "Jack-of-all-trades" though not necessarily the master of none. What they fail to understand is that the job description carries with it the Christian challenge of being responsible for both the temporal and spiritual needs of the lonely client, who is not considered a bona fide member of the rat race civilization anymore. Not to mention that most of the time, it pays much better with a lot of perks (free room and board, tissue paper and toilet articles included; Christmas and birthday bonuses; workmen's compensation coverage, free tickets to cultural shows with the client in tow; etc.) and with less pressure than working as an administrative assistant in an office. Or, it could even be a pleasant starting point for an immigrant who is still trying to fit into the local working force, a welcome respite from a former demanding organizational structure. A friend of mine in LA was already included in the will of her ward, an honor, she maintained, she simply deserved what with wiping off her old lady's butt for five years and her money being green. Another relative, a high-caliber professional in the Phil, was blessed to be bequethed by her jeweller client eleven genuine silver dollars amounting to S60,000 - S70,000, which were more than enough to send her two kids to college aside from birthstones and other expensive china wares she was made to choose from among said client's personal collection. Or, a client's family who, upon the death of their mom, gave her caregiver two months' separation pay as a cash reward aside from the letter of commendation vouching her integrity and moral character for her next employer-to-be. And to top it all, I could never have written this memoir had I settled for another job, not that of a caregiver.

"What! You a professor at a big university in Manila and here you'd be a maid again!" My aunt commented unmaliciously when she learned of my plan.

"I don't give a damn!" I replied having in mind the dignity of labor, one of the values taught to us by my father, aside from the fact that what I was earning for a month as a "molder of the youths" in my native land I could get here for only a day in the "land of Uncle Sam," peso-wise.

IV

Life with Dr. Domini

Dr. Domini at 67 still had that sturdy build of an Italian golf professional and looked the same as when I saw him last in 1996. This I could see as he stepped out of the sleek blue Mercedes Benz he was driving when he and his sister came to fetch me from a friend's house where I usually stayed when I was in Sunnyvale. They both gave me a hug of welcome and after exchanging pleasantries with my sister, who had driven me from San Francisco, we started off for Dr. Domini's new house in a plush suburb within the city area. A few months ago, he had successfully sold his old sprawling 10-room house with a swimming pool. It was there where we stayed with Rose, his mom, when I first worked for them.

"Big house but no wife, no kids," Rose used to taunt him.

"But, Mom, I don't have plans to replace the only woman in my life," he used to answer her, referring to his beautiful and charming wife who died ten years ago of breast cancer.

Sometimes when Rose and I would sit in the terrace overlooking the scenic spot before us, she would confide in me saying, "How I wish my son would get a wife to keep his house spic and span and take care of him."

"Well, he doesn't need a wife, Rose. All that he needs is a maid," I would answer her. It took me several months to be comfortable in calling her by her first name, which Dr. Domini wanted me to do, another unthinkable scenario in the Philippines, where to do so would offend the receiver of your message 43 years your senior, who would reprimand you saying your parents must have forgotten to teach you GMRC (called "good manners and right conduct" during my time, later referred to as "deportment").

Dr. Domini's new house this time was also big. It was a nine-room, two-level house you could reach five minutes after you had identified yourself and passed the guarded main entrance to the private subdivision. Three houses away from his own was a unique architectural design, he told me, owned by a football player earning a whooping seven-figure salary playing quarterback for his team. I told him that it is not a surprise knowing that in this country, teachers and other professionals earn just peanuts compared to what an athlete gets whose potentials are more brawn than brains.

Dr. Domini's three children with their families were waiting for us, ditto with Mayette, his girlfriend of six months he was telling me about when he called me in Manila. She was a widow but still attractive and chic at 54, a farmer from Pleasanton who would drive all the way just to visit Dr. Domini, most weekends spending the night at his place. She would also bring us fresh produce from her farm like sweet corn and fist-sized peaches which he would in turn share generously with the two of his children living nearby.

"If I marry again, Mom, I'll get a rich lady," I remembered Dr. Domini kid his mom when we were still in Sunnyvale.

I was sure the lady in question at that time was thrilled to find herself receiving an approval of my boss' chauvinistic affection. That night, we had a happy reunion at the subdivision's clubhouse where Dr. Domini treated us to a festive dinner.

"What! But that's a sin!" Rose was seething with rage when she learned the next day that Mayette spent the night in Dr. Domini's room. She told me she had a hunch the two just did not talk about the birds and the bees. Being Italian and a devout Catholic at that she was shocked when she knew that her dear son she presumed celibate and chaste after his wife's demise had his feet of clay, having forgotten that she was now living in the twentieth century, when what she used to believe to be the proper code of decorum where faith and morals are concerned was now passé.

"Oh, don't worry, your son is over 21, Rose, and for sure, he will just go to confession this weekend before receiving comunion, which he does every Sunday, " I laughingly appeased her as she was getting ready to storm Dr. Domini's room to "give him a piece of my mind." I was scared she might have a heart attack as to what she might see there.

Dr. Domini could not look at us straight to the eyes across the breakfast table that morning. "Mayette left earlier," he simply said.

He himself looked pretty smug like every inch a contented, drenched cow.

V

Reaching for a Chip in Silicon Valley

Just like before in Sunnyvale, Rose and I shared one bedroom complete with bath. We ate our meals together because Dr. Domini was out of the house most of the time, either at his office or with his buddies at the golf course inside the subdivision. We said our rosary together before going to bed at night. In the morning, she greeted me with her usual, "Oh, why didn't God take me away?" to which I said, "Rose, you should be thankful to the Lord for giving you the gift of life which not all people have every day of their lives. Some do not even wake up anymore but go on sleeping forever."

While staying with Dr. Domini and Rose, my cousins and friends encouraged me to apply for a teaching job at the diocese of San Jose, which fills up working positions in all Catholic schools within their area of responsibility. Dr. Domini himself was kind enough to request his daughter to make a computerized resumé for me, the credibility of which was augmented by two letters of recommendation from him and a former schoolmate in college who is now a successful lawyer in the area. The day after I mailed the necessary credentials to the office of the diocese, there was a call from a Catholic nun in Gilroy who asked me some preliminary questions on a job interview but after finding out that I got my degrees in the Philippines, (a Bachelor of Arts major in English and Political Science with special units in Journalism, Magna Cum Laude and a Master in Public Administration where I was consistently on the dean's list) she turned me down. A case of cultural discrimination?

To the bio-data I faxed as a response to their ad in the newspaper, the head of a language center in the city teaching English as a second language (ESL) offered me a four-hour/day,three-days-a-week job because he told me on the phone they were in dire need of a foreign-trained English professor to teach Vietnamese students who have just arrived in the US. It being a part-time job only, I decided not to accept it because I needed a full-time position to justify my application for adjustment of status with Immigration.

Keeping my mind focused along this line also helped me not to miss my family so much although most nights, I'd cry myself to sleep thinking about them. Calling them up twice a month simply could not assuage my longing for them. Oh, well, in life you can't have everything. You can have one but must give up the other, and I was at this point in time resolved not to let anything divert me while I pressed on towards my goal.

Before Rose was scheduled to return to LA the first week of August, Dr. Domini planned a family cruise to celebrate her 91st birthday to take place August of next year. I was included in the party with his mom and myself to share a cabin, all expenses paid. Mayette would be ensconced in his and never mind if his mom raised her eyebrows. Although I looked upon this kind of activity as an idle way of spending your extra bucks when all you would get are ten pounds of excess body weight the moment you get off the ship, I had to politely accept the invitation.

It was also at this time that a cousin-in-law showed me a letter from his wife's (my cousin) friend working at Long Beach and petitioned by her employer on a working visa. She even gave him the address of the agency in the same city handling her case and after much deliberation, I decided to call them up to inquire. They, in return, advised me to see them at their office located in the financial district of the city and to bring along all my credentials.

I also called up my husband's older sister in Inglewood in LA county, who was more than glad to accommodate and help me get started in the next chapter of my life.

The night before Dr. Domini was to drive his mom back to Anaheim and my last night with them, he called me to his study (which I teasingly call in his presence his "oval office") and thanked me personally for the good service I did for him and his mom. He even reminded me about our cruise next year and to make myself available then. Before we parted ways, he gave me two envelopes: one, he said, was my pay for that month and the other, my bonus and parting gift. When I opened the second envelope, I was surprised but happy to find four new, crisp $100 bills. Enough to cover the processing fee of my job hunting spree in LA, which he did not have the slightest idea of.

Believing that things just don't happen but they are

caused, I asked myself if this was a sign from Somebody up there telling me that I was on the right track and needed not be afraid to step into the dark but have faith and trust in Him.

VI

Stark Realities in LA Circa 1997

The all-Filipino staff of our employment agency at Long Beach was very warm and accommodating to us applicants for an office job who were paired off with our prospective employer-petitioners. The manager-owner of the office, a pleasant and debonair gentleman who was formerly a lawyer in Manila, oriented us as regards their standard operation procedure within the context of immigration laws to help us eventually adjust our status. Although they also have applicants from other countries, he specifically boosted our morale telling us that most employers asking for employees would always ask him, "Could you send us a Filipino applicant?" Filipino workers, he said, are noted to be efficient not to mention that they don't have the so-called language barrier, thanks to the fact that in the Philippines, English is considered our second language, it being the medium of instruction in our schools so that even our street vendors speak and understand it. I remembered how Mayette, Dr. Domini's girlfriend, appeared surprised when she heard me speak straight English and use high-sounding terms, for she was not expecting it from one who comes from a third world country, at which point I suggested tactfully she look it up in the dictionary.

Our processing fee was $400, which we had to pay up front and in full (thanks to what Dr. Domini gave me as my bonus and parting gift). We also had to sign a contract with our co-maker (my brother-in-law who was with me that time) stating among other things that upon placement on the job we were referred to, we had to pay our agency 10 percent of our monthly salary for the next ten months. Then, we were made to understand that the moment our employer signs our petition papers, which is discretionary on his part, the same will be forwarded to the agency's immigration lawyer who, for $1,800 and covered by another contract which provided that we have to shell out 40 percent only as initial payment and the balance to be paid equally on a monthly installment, will start to work on our application prior to its submission to Immigration for processing. If nothing goes awry (which the owner-manager of the office assured us is always the case), we could have our working visa after three months. By then, we could already sponsor a thanksgiving mass for breathing freely and walking off the tightrope unlike before when we always have to be on the lookout for immigration officers who, on a tip, might raid any workplace. They could subject to outright deportation proceedings those caught without the necessary work authorization and penalize the employer as a consequence. The much sought-after working visa is good for three years, renewable for another three years, the same number of years we have to sweat it out as chattels by neccesity to satisfy our employer who has the upper hand and would determine our destiny.

Holy mackerel, I muttered to myself as I made a mental calculation of the figures involved, I could already be in a financial quagmire even before I could get to start off earning my daily bread. Then, how about other incidental expenses to keep my body and soul together? And I still don't have any idea as to how much monthly pay I can negotiate with my would-be employer. However, inasmuch as I already had gone this far, I braced myself saying, "It's now or never!"

The first employer I was sent to for a job interview was a Vietnamese entrepreneur in the textile business. He seemed to be a kind family man who proudly displayed some framed photos of his wife and kids on his desk while he oriented me as to my job title (secretary) and job description (customer service, mail and communication and other related activities - no coffee making for him or his business associates who might drop by and for which I was thankful, considering it to be unprofessional, my brain being suited for things more than that). It was, he further said, a Monday-Friday job from 8 AM – 5 PM with a one- hour break from 12 Noon-1 PM and paying $7.50 an hour (an "under-the-table" deal or tax-free), a little more than the $5.75 an hour minimum wage here in California. I was to start the next day if it was fine with me. Also, he would sign my petition papers three months after if things turn out okay with our working relationship, which was not the case because on the third day he called me to his office telling me his Vietnamese clients complained they could not understand me on the phone. The negative assessment was simply mutual because their language was Greek to me, too. He gave me my three-day pay, which I found out after opening the envelope that he computed it only at $6.50 an hour and when I questioned him about it, he justified his action saying that was the rate he gave me (which was not what we had agreed upon verbally when he accepted me) inasmuch as I still did not have my working permit. I was shocked to know that he ripped me off, a clear case of labor exploitation, and upon regaining my composure told myself it must have been a "blessing in disguise" in that it would have been worse if it was after three months. When I referred the matter to the agency, they told me they can't do anything to help in the situation because all personnel issues like job title, job description, wage rate, working hours, and the like are between the employer and the employee themselves. As long as they can have the 10 percent of our monthly salary, we have to fend for ourselves. It takes two to tango, it's true, but I found out that in this situation "the boss may be wrong but he's still the boss."

My second job was in Torrance with a real estate office managed by a couple, a Canadian realtor and his Filipino wife, the latter being the senior vice-president of the office. She was smart but kind and assured me she could help with my papers. I was designated customer service manager and in order to augment my $8 an hour entry-level rate before taxes, I was allowed to do overtime services checking on our clients with delayed payments to the office. With my background in journalism and experience in having been a staff member of an office publication in Manila, I was also assigned to take care of the in-house newsletter with an "off-the-record" assignment of being the SVP's "ghost writer." I enjoyed the freedom my new job offered me as we took our clients and would-be buyers on all-expenses paid trips to the company-owned lands in Nevada and Arizona with overnight hotel accommodations usually at Laughlin where gambling went on for twenty-four hours a day, seven days a week. It was also here that I learned to do escrow work, which was not a part of real estate business in my country.

As part of the office staff taking care that the meetings twice a week with our agents and finders (these are the unlicensed agents), which took place after office hours and ended up late at night be successful, my bosses decided to look for a place for me to stay in the city rather than go home everyday to Inglewood (where I was staying with my in-laws). Luckily, one of our finders, Mina, who originally came from Guam, had a two-bedroom apartment unit on the eighth floor of a hotel building that was just a five-minute walk from our office. She was more than glad enough to take me in. One of the bedrooms was rented to a Japanese administrative assistant and her American boyfriend, Ken, a computer analyst who Mina assured me was a "harmless" guy we could trust. Mina (a certified nursing assistant here in the US for fifteen years now but who has not adjusted her status yet); Lanie (separated from her husband in Mexico and worked as a housekeeper for $7 an hour, eight hours a day and five days a week and also undocumented) and I occupied the other. With "Barbie" (what we mischievously call our Japanese roommate) paying $400 for her room with Ken, Lanie and I chipping in $200 each, Mina was practically rent-free with $200 more for her pocket money, being the landlady of our $600 per month apartment unit. All five of us had an individual key to the unit and it was an "each monkey to his own branch" setup but we all got along pretty fine with no hassle, or so I thought. Mina and Lanie, when off from their work, were seldom home and would go ballroom dancing every Friday night to "unwind" with their circle of friends, some of whom have spouses and grown-up children left in their home countries, but settled for other equally "lonely" partners here in the US, their moral values thrown out to the winds, maintaining that "if you are in Rome, do what the Romans do." My roommates would also invite me to go with them but I would tell them I'd rather stay home and read.

Once a week, together with their once Catholic friends but now converted to the "Born Again" fellowship, they would hold a prayer meeting in our unit and although I helped them in the kitchen prepare their food for their "sharing of the bread" afterwards, I never joined them in their activity and they respected me for that. You can be in the world although not of the world, right?

It was in this scenario that I came to know a couple, Bong and May, and their rather pathetic stories.Bong, an active community leader in Manila, came to the US on a tourist visa three years ahead of his wife, May. He had decided to "look for a greener pasture" here in the "land of Uncle Sam" when their fishing business in Navotas, a coastal town in the Phil., went bankrupt. Eighteen months after arriving in California and finalizing his "divorce" papers in Reno(a prearranged plan with May while still in Manila), he was introduced to Dory, a US citizen five years his senior who consented to "marry" him for $5,000 (a "fixed" marriage), with the agreement that she will petition him for adjustment of his status; $3,000 payable upon filing of the necessary papers with Immigration, whose fees were naturally shouldered by Bong himself and the balance to be paid upon temporary approval of the petition. Another verbal "pre-nuptial" agreement was for Bong to pay for the apartment unit located two floors below ours, their domicile as far as Immigration is concerned which is alleged to conduct an on-the-spot checking even at the most unholy hour. Dory and her 18-year old son who is gay occupied one of the two bedrooms of the unit while Bong and May (when she arrived later), the other. The poor fellow had to practise "poverty by choice" most of the time and be contented with second-hand clothes he bought from Goodwill or other thrift stores. He had to work as a security guard during the day and as a caregiver at night to pay all their bills (food, electricity, water, and telephone), which are officially under his and Dory's names - again, another facade to satisfy Immigration as to the veracity of their conjugal relationship. All these ordeals Bong had to accept willy-nilly until such time that he could get hold of his "green card" which will take not less than three years.

"If not for my Christian belief, I could have killed these SOBs," Bong confided to me one time after their fellowship's prayer meeting.

May, on the other hand, was lucky enough to have found a job immediately upon arrival in California, also as a tourist. She was a live-in caregiver to a 90-year-old lady for $1,000 a month, Monday-Friday. On weekends, she went home to Bong's apartment unit. "Divorced" from Bong, she was able to contract another "fixed" marriage with Lito, a former neighbor in Manila for the same amount Bong paid to Dory; she had also to maintain another apartment for Lito with some of her clothes and other personal effects stored in his closet to make it appear they are living together as husband and wife in case Immigration comes knocking at their door. Aside from taking care of their bills, May had to provide Lito a monthly allowance that enabled him to bum around without a care in this world, not bothering to work, which he bragged he did not need to do, what with a "sugar mommy," anyway. Just like Bong, she had to force herself to adjust to the set-up until getting her much coveted "green card," too.

But Bong and May were in a better situation than Otilia, Dr. Domini's Guatemalan cleaning lady (for five years and paid $50 for an eight-hour job, twice a month) who was blackmailed by her "paid" Latino husband threatening to report her to Immigration if she would not give in to his demand for sex (not included in their initial verbal agreement) in addition to his food, clothing, and shelter she was paying for, leaving her almost nothing to send to her family in Guatemala.

It was also at this time that I had an experience which I'm sure had it not been for Somebody up there and my guardian angel, I might have been a victim of an unsolved crime in a country not mine.

One fine morning, clad in my robe and walking towards our bathroom to take a shower before leaving for the office (Mina and Lanie had left earlier), I heard Ken shouting for help in their room. I was surprised to know that he was still around (I seldom saw him get out of their room) and my being a "Good Samaritan" getting the better of me, I pushed open their door which was ajar. All the while, what was on my mind was that he might have had an accident or suffered a stroke and needed help immediately but I got the shock of my life when I saw him all naked, huddled at one end of their walk-in closet and masturbating !

"Oh, my God!" My mouth was open literally. We always have a "first" in all things in life but definitely this was the worst among my worse firsts.

"No, don't leave!" He ordered me when he saw I was about to get out of their room.

Keeping my cool under pressure (thanks to the discipline I learned from our Debate and Argumentation class in college) so as to maintain presence of mind, I tried to appear relaxed. I also remembered what I read in a psychology book that a manifestation like Ken's is a form of exhibitionism and that one who encounters such a person should not panic, be embarassed, or insult him so as not to further excite him, which might lead him to do a murderous action. I also took stock of the fact that our apartment unit being at the eighth floor, it was possible that after raping and killing me, he could throw my body down the building making it appear I committed suicide and there being no eyewitness to the crime, he could go scot-free.

"Okay, Ken, what can I do to help?" I smiled at him condescendingly, all the time praying, "Mama Mary, please help me!"

"Oh, nothing. Just keep me company," he was saying all the time that he was trying to relieve himself. I found his action rather beastly and I avoided looking at him.

Boy, that was the longest one and a half hours of my life. I had to think of all topics under the sun (he was making sexual innuendoes all the time but I had to deviate it) just to keep our conversation going on smoothly. I also had to let him presume that he was simply doing a "normal" thing. However, I had noted that there was one subject matter he did not want to discuss and that was about his family. Then, when I thought I had gained his trust and confidence, I reminded him casually that I had to get going for I might be late for work. After much consideration, he allowed me to leave their room.

When I got out of the bathroom after my much-needed shower (I was singing to myself to take my mind off from that rather horrendous incident a few minutes ago), I again saw Ken without a stitch on eyeing me from the door of their room.

"Ken, don't you think it would be best for you to cover yourself up? It's cold and you might get pneumonia aside from the fact that some people in the next building would be horrified to see you in all your glory." I smiled at him sweetly but unprovocatively before going inside our room, locking it after me. When I came out of it later, all dressed up for the office, he was still there; he did not budge but just kept on looking at me with that same expression he had before.

Up to now, I still can't figure out how I managed to be as cool as a cucumber when one small mistake in my brain's decision-making compartment could have brought me to a tragic end. But one thing I was aware of; Somebody up there loves me so much that He freed me from the clutches of the devil.

"Hey, you're okay?" One of my companions asked me solicitously when he noticed me grab at one of the two bars inside the elevator that was taking us down to the first floor.

My knees were shaking uncontrollably and most probably, he had noticed me turn pale - a delayed reaction.

"I'm okay, thanks." I appreciated his concern for me.

One could wonder at the dual nature of man and how it could change suddenly from evil to good.

"Mama mia! We have a maniac in the house!" Lanie shrieked that night when I related to them what happened to me the day before.

"It's good he did not touch you." Mina was genuinely concerned.

"Thanks for the sympathy, guys, but don't you envy me? At least I saw Ken's everything! It was a privilege he did not extend to you," I retorted laughingly.

VII

A Tribe Divided

If a thing is not meant for you, there will be glitches but there must be a reason for such, the perennial "why" behind the action. This I found out after working for three months at the real estate office. That was the time when I was looking forward to having our senior vice president (SVP) sign my petition papers for my H-1 B (working) visa when one day, she called me to her office to tell me that our senior officer (who was next in rank to her) had handed in her letter of irrevocable resignation. I was to make a press release about it (when *I* joined the staff, I never suspected trouble brewing between the two of them because outwardly, they appeared to be the best of friends, both working on the "management-by-objectives" principle). But that was just the tip of the iceberg because a couple of days after, we received numerous calls and letters from our clients signifying their desire to discontinue the monthly amortization for the properties they had been paying for years because of financial difficulties and requesting reimbursement for payments made to the office which, if it allowed, will put the office in a financial imbroglio. As customer service manager, I was also under pressure because I had to cover up for the SVP who sometimes did not want to take calls directed to her and which got the ire of those in the opposite camp who we suspected were under the tutelage of our former senior officer. Realizing the tight fix I was in, I saw that the possibility of having me petitioned by my boss was quite remote.

When I presented my problem to the manager of our agency, he asked me if I wanted to change jobs, I readily agreed and upon acceptance at my new office, I went back to my former job site to signify my intention of resigning from my position, which was further justified when the SVP gave me an unsigned letter addressed to me. The gist was a threat to report me to Immigration for working without the necessary permit; it would consequently penalize my employer for hiring me.

And I thought that we Filipinos had discarded one of our negative cultural traits, our so-called "crab mentality" (not wanting a fellow Filipino to succeed in life or finding a foothold in his climb to prosperity), which definitely hampers us from moving up the economic ladder here in America. We have Chinatown and Japantown but not yet a Filipinotown. Furthermore, we are commended internationally as resilient people with a lot of ingenuity in many areas so it is a $64 question why we can't work for unity instead of division. If we could, we could be an ethnic group to reckon with in the American society.

My next job was administrative assistant in a big bookstore in Long Beach, my employer this time was a Nicaraguan lady who migrated from Nicaragua as a teenager and

divorced from her husband who, she told me during our first
encounter, she discovered to be gay. Upon learning that I
have three kids in Manila, she boasted that she got pregnant
twice by two different men but had abortions just to get rid
of "them." It was "too bothersome" for her, she emphasized,
sounding as if she was just discarding some useless toys. Her
perspective on the sacredness of life gave me goose pimples.
She also had a flair for using gutter language because she
found it sophisticated.

I was busy doing my boss' correspondence on my second
day at her office when my phone rang.

"Hi! Is Marina there?" said the caller at the other end of
the line after I had initiated the usual telephone courtesy.

"I'm sorry but she's out of the office at the moment.
Could I just take a message, please?"

"Hey, you're Filipino, right. I am, too. Listen, I once
worked for Marina and it was a nightmare I haven't gotten
over yet. Nobody there stays for more than a week and I
bet ditto with you," the prophetess of doom delivered her
message in a bombshell before hanging up.

True to my unidentified caller's warning, I found out
my latest employer was impossible to work for. She took
note of the number of times you went in and out of the
restroom reminding you how much money she has to pay
for the water you flushed there; called her cashier "bitch"
behind her back while being all smiles when she faced her (I
suspected I was given the same treatment); wasn't bothered
a bit if you had indigestion because she expected you to
be working during your lunch break and other eccentric
policies she wanted to impose just because she believed

she was the boss and infallible, just like the Pope when speaking ex-cathedra.

I left after working for her for just four days, more than enough time to maintain my equilibrium.

But there was one thing I was thankful for, which I considered a blessing while working with Marina and that was meeting and getting acquainted with two of her friends. How, I was wondering, could they get along fine with her when they have different sets of values? It was an exceptional case when oil and water could mix, and unfathomable for me.

Manny and Chi, a down-to-earth couple married for twenty years with two great kids, headed an active charismatic group in the heart of Long Beach - the former, working as a finance officer of a big hospital also in the city, is an accomplished musician; the latter, an insurance consultant, has leadership skill aside from being a dusky beauty herself who one time was a "Mrs. Cavite-LA." Chi, always a generous soul, invited me to stay with them upon knowing that I was looking for a place after that horrendous incident with Ken. I did not have second thoughts when I accepted her invitation specially, when I saw a chapel at the first floor of their rented house where we had mass now and then. It was here that I met Dan, a divorced Filipino green card holder who was a regular participant in their weekly prayer meeting. Several times, Chi would kiddingly insinuate Dan could be a good prospect if I wanted to adjust my status through marriage and of course, she was more than willing to play Cupid for us especially when Dan made it obvious he wanted to start more than an ordinary friendship with me. I discouraged him tactfully. I knew Chi's intention was good but I made my point clear, graciously maintaining, "What profits a man if he owns the whole world but suffers the loss of his own soul?" I added I never would be willing to sell my soul to the highest bidder. There could be other options, anyway; it is not yet the end of the world.

My last job at LA was with a textile factory where I was in charge of customer service with access to the computer in updating the records of our sales representatives in the field. There were seven of us, all ladies, in the clerical pool: four Filipinos and the three daughters of the Russian owner of the firm, the eldest acting as manager of our office and a very nice lady at that. Inasmuch as I was new to the job, I was supposed to be trained by another Filipino co-worker who was the most senior among the four of us. She had been connected with a bank in Manila and now was a green card holder having been petitioned by our employer three years before.

"I'm known to be the 'queen' in this working area," she said when I sat down with her to start my on-the-job training. Wanting to establish rapport with everyone from the very start and my nature being it doesn't bother me a bit if a person feels and thinks he is the master of the universe as long as he does not impose his megalomania on me, I simply smiled, thinking she was just pulling my leg but this was disproven later on when, during our lunch break which the "queen" does not join in because we are not "in" with her crowd, my other two Filipino co-workers affirmed her presumption of grandeur. In order to maintain a peaceful co-existence among them, both of them decided to take the line of "least resistance," that is, to kowtow to the "queen's" whims and caprices "If you can't lick 'em, join 'em"?.

History repeated itself. I left after a week despite my boss' daughters' pleas to reconsider my decision and our manager suggesting to continue my training with her. With the "queen" still on her perch in the same working area with me, it would be a case of "too many chiefs but not too many Indians".

I also learned from a very reliable grapevine that the lady before me who was also trained by her left after less than a week.

"I'd rather work with other nationalities than somebody from my own country. That way, there would not be any hassle, intrigue, or back stabbing." I remembered what Eden, my cousin working as the only Filipino staff member of a Japanese firm in San Diego for fifteen years now, had told me.She was right.

VIII

Unexpected Nemeses in Sacramento

It was in mid-January of 1998 when I came to a decision after assessing my situation in Long Beach. It seemed that my attempt to adjust my status through a working visa was not going in any direction because somewhere, somehow, there was always something along the way to make it flop. It was also at this time that my mother (a naturalized US citizen who had been reluctant before to adjust her status) filed a petition for me under a special immigration law, a petition which was consequently approved without much ado, my security blanket while I'm here in corporate America.

Readjusting my priorities in my hierarchy of needs this time, I called up Sophie, a close family friend in Sacramento, who with her husband, Gerry, maintained a carehome in the city. I told her my predicament and presented my proposal: I would help them in their carehome without any salary while on a job-hunting spree in the capital city of California. It was an on-the-spot acceptance with a mutual interest at hand - a week after I arrived, Gerry and Sophie left for a two-week cruise leaving their carehome under my care and supervision with six elderly clients mostly in a world of their own. I also found out that had I not made that frantic call from LA, they could have cancelled their trip because they had no one to leave their business with. It was clearly a situation where one's desperation is another's godsend.

I never received a "Thank you" from them. They enjoyed their R and R (rest and recreation) at my expense, free of charge. Charge it to experience? Nor was there an acknowledgement for those free services I provided, helping them during the weekends. When I was free from my job, they could then go home to their residence in the suburbs at night with me to face any contingency affecting the primary source of their income.

Oh, well, life is sometimes unfair but what can you do …?

Another input for my "black box," an imaginary box in my head where I stockpile my unpleasant memories.

My first client this time was a 45-year old guy with multiple sclerosis (MS) who accepted me on the phone after I had read his ad in the local newspaper. He had been bedridden for the past ten years and divorced from his wife even before the onset of his disability. My job description called for helping him with his personal necessities, medication, and food planning and preparation, all for a measly sum of $200 per week although I had my own room complete with bath in addition to free food, the usual amenities for a live-in job. I decided to stick it out with him while still looking for another job with higher pay, which was topmost among my priorities this time. He had his son and the son's fiancee living with us with their separate food cabinet but I found it hard to believe (probably due to my conservative Filipino upbringing) that they never bothered to say "hello" to the sick man in the two weeks that I was with them when their room was right next to his, he could even hear their squeals at night either of agony or ecstasy.

I also remembered a similar case I was exposed to last 1995 when I worked as a reliever for a lady also with MS for twenty-five years. Her only child, a daughter, and her boyfriend were staying with us under one roof and would pass by my client's room every time they went to the bathroom but never bothered to talk to her. They doted more on their pet iguana in their room. It was so big it scared the wits out of me. I had to check that their room was always closed when they were away during the day.

My next employer, Shariff, was of African-American descent originally from Nigeria. My client this time was a 30-year-old DD (developmentally disabled) lady in a wheelchair whose personality profile showed her to be a menopausal baby. When she was just 18, she was placed by her parents in an institution for her kind until last year when she was transferred to my employer's carehome. I also learned for the first time that a case like this is subsidized by the government, which made me understand how in this country, progressive and rich as it is, an ob-gyne will just advise an expectant mother in her 40s (a late pregnancy) to resort to an abortion because of possible abnormalities on the part of the fetus, hence, when born will just be a liability rather than an asset to the state. Furthermore, what makes this level of care different (it is a one-on-one) is that the caregiver had to make a nightly report on the client's behavioral attitude to be discussed with her case manager once a month for assessment of the case.

It was also in this scenario when I found out how choice of words could have contextual differences and one's naivete could break the monotony of a rather dull life.

One day, Shariff requested a friend of his, also of African-American descent, to drive me downtown to complete the credentials needed for my job. While in the car, he told me he is divorced with two kids staying with him. I told him that I am very much married with my husband and three kids still in Manila and even showed him my wedding ring which I always wear and never hide, unlike some people with hidden agenda. Nevertheless, my status did not deter him from asking me to go out with him and he was rather adamant about it. Considering his kindness when he accommodated me in securing my papers and wanting to be simply cordial towards him being my boss' friend, I told him, "I'll check my schedule first." He also gave me his phone number which I threw away surreptitiously afterwards.

For a week, he pestered me with his morning calls, which he made when he knew Shariff was away. As always, I would ward him off with my "I'm busy", thinking that he would get the message right and clear and back off. When I told Gerry about it, he explained that here in the US, saying,"I'll check my schedule first" is tantamount to your being open to the guy's invitation and that if you mean "no," then, say "NO!" and stick to your guns.

"I bet if you'd go out on a date with him and the lights went out, you'd be playing hide and seek with each other because you can't even see his teeth at all," Gerry's brother, who had a sadistic sense of humor, chipped in while we were having dinner that night. That elicited guffaw from the rest of us. I had to give him a playful kick from under the table to give him a dose of his own medicine.

"So, how's our date? Have you already scheduled it?" My "Pygmalion" sounded so complacent on the phone when he called me up again the next day. I was just thinking that men who assume they are doing us a favor when they invite us out simply prove they are a bunch of chauvinistic pigs that deserve to be skinned alive.

"Hey, look here. I'm flattered with the attention you're giving me but I'd like to tell you this - I don't have any intention of scheduling a date with you and never will because I'm married and happily at that so I'd appreciate it if you'd stop calling me, okay?"

I never heard from him anymore after that day much to my relief, nor did I see his shadow at my boss' house which was also a change.

So much for lesson number 2 where men are concerned.

It dawned on me that one could have a dozen kids yet remain innocent though not necessarily ignorant to the ways of the world.

If I almost got raped and possibly killed in Torrance, I almost got the latter in Sacramento.

Shariff and his American wife have an eight-year old cute girl, Mikki, and when the latter reported to her 7 PM - 4 AM job at a local factory, she dropped Mikki off at our carehome to play with our client until her father came to pick her up which was around 10 or 11 in the evening. I did not mind so much the extra babysitting job without any pay inasmuch as I enjoyed the little girl's company. She reminded me of MC, my own daughter, when she was her age.

That fateful evening, my client and I were already sound asleep (Shariff wanted me to leave my room open at all times but I asserted I wanted my own privacy and anyway, I had always been a light sleeper and could still hear my client's movement in her own room) when I heard a loud knocking at my door.

"Where's Mikki?" He asked me without any protocol at all. He smelled of liquor.

"She was watching TV a while ago when I left her. She told me to just go to bed while waiting for you," I explained, still a little bit disoriented.

"She's not around! Where's she?" He was already shrieking.

"Now, hold it! Why don't you compose yourself?" I tried to keep my cool so that I could control the situation.

"If my daughter got lost, I'll kill you!" And in that moment, I saw not the face of a rational man but the blazing eyes of the devil against his black countenance. So, he'd murder me if something happened to the apple of his eye, my foot, when in fact before his wife confided to me how he wanted her to abort Mikki when she was just a tadpole in her womb because he was not yet ready at that time to face the responsibilities of fatherhood. It's good that her maternal instinct to have a baby at any cost got the better of her realizing that her biological clock was ticking fast.

I was not intimidated by his chilling threat but looked at him straight to the eyes and with a soft but determined voice declared, "Shariff, this is America, not Nigeria. Do you understand?!"

How a soft answer could turn away wrath and could douse what was a short while ago the blazing ember of an emotional outburst.

It was an eyeball-to-eyeball situation, both of us waiting to see who would blink first when the door opened and his wife came in with Mikki in tow. Putting two and two together, she explained to him that a few minutes ago, she came over to pick up Mikki (she left the factory earlier because of a headache, she said) but on the spur of the moment, decided to drive back realizing that she had not told me about it. She apologized profusely when I told her Shariff almost killed me upon finding Mikki nowhere to be found. Shariff did the same thing, too, for his rather impulsive outburst but it did not stop me from handing him my letter of resignation the next day.

That was another close shave but I managed to come out unscathed. St. Peter up there must be saying, "It's not yet your time, Meriam, so stay put."

IX

Life's Bitter Blows

1998 was another memorable year. 1979 was the year I got married at Hilton Hotel, a 5-star hotel in Manila; 1980, the birth of Arnold, my eldest son, followed by my daughter, MC, in 1981. "Mrs. Dela Cruz, again!" exclaimed the head nurse at the delivery room when she recognized me being wheeled in. She had also assisted me the year before. Fr. Constancio Gan, that good Vincentian priest and my spiritual director who married us in 1979, baptized Arnold in 1980 and during MC's baptismal party a year after admonished Rudy and me good-naturedly saying, "Better practice family planning so that you can play tennis more." Then he baptized Albert in 1984 (I did not know I was pregnant until I felt some dizzy spells in between our practice for that year's government corporation athletic association ladies lawn tennis tournament where I was playing with our office team that I had to quit for fear he might come out long before his time), the last two being Lamaze babies (Rudy and I took Lamaze lessons during the eighth month of my pregnancy with MC and he was right there with me at the delivery room witnessing the miracle of birth which I think is the most effective way of family planning globally).

It was in May of that year when I received news that my dear father died of complications of the heart in the Philippines where he had gone home for good three months before. He and my mother came to the US in 1980 upon my older sister's petition and after retiring from the government service in our country - he, as a public school principal who was willing to forego a meal just to read his favorite *Philippine Free Press*, a popular news magazine in the Philippines before the martial law, which had the penchant for reporting both domestic and international events objectively; she, as a music and art teacher in the elementary school of our town, who, we kidded before, could run and win a seat in local politics hands down because of the sure support of her former pupils from all walks of life, from the fish and vegetable vendors in the market to the mayor. We marvelled at how she enjoyed the tiresome job of being the chair of every musical program now and then that one time, she was asked if she's a widow because they haven't seen a "Mr. Baniel" (my father shunned public limelight). And if other people would want a "No Visitors Allowed" sign to be hung in their room when they are sick, my mother found entertaining the guests who frequented our house a panacea for her recurring headaches.

The six of us - my only brother (an agriculturist who also worked with the Philippine government before retiring) and four other sisters (three registered nurses here in the US and our eldest, a master teacher II still in the Phil.) were all brought up in a rather conservative household, where the emphases were on academic excellence by my mother (consequently attested by the ribbons and medals we earned in school) and formation of Christian moral values by example by my father. He inculcated in us honesty and humility in our professional life and believed in taking even the last shirt off his back to one he thought needed it more than he. From him, I learned my early lessons of sharing, the condiment that gives meaning to life, not only your surplus (which most of the time is the common thing with some people) but even though it hurts.

Another moral lesson he imparted to us was the joy in living a rather simple life that not even several years of staying here in America where he was exposed to all forms of consumerism changed him a bit. In a way, I think he was right in saying that practicing poverty by choice is one healthy stress-reduction regimen; say, having just three sets of clothes (formal, informal, and indoor) is a better situation than having a dozen in your closet which will give you a headache in narrowing down your choice as to which one is the best among the crop.

"Just be contented with what you have and don't go to the extent of incurring debts just to keep up with the Joneses," he used to remind us.

All throughout his waking hours, my father practised the "waste not, want not" philosophy of Mother Teresa, although he had not heard nor read about her yet. He never threw anything away because he said it might come handy when you need it most. More so while he was in the U.S. where material goods are superfluous. He enjoyed taking long walks and would pick up whatever empty soda cans he could find along the way and stuff them in a plastic bag that was always in his pocket, step on them to flatten them, and when he had stocked up a lot in the bin at the garage of their rented house with my mother he would bring them to a Safeway outlet to be exchanged for grocery coupons.

"What! You a principal here in the Phil, and there you are in America picking up garbage? You better come home quick and fast!" My brother roared with anger when he learned and before he understood about my father's latest entrepreneurial past time, something he had in common with many ambulatory elderly of the city.

I never could beat my father at the tennis court when we played singles (they used to be tennis partners with my mother during their younger days), his potshots being very tricky. I could also confide in him things I could not tell my mother and got a reminder, not a reprimand (especially during those days when I was a student activist and our bunch was the idealistic type with an invisible halo in our head), he was both a father and pal to me.

Anyway, one evening shortly after his death when I was saying my rosary for the eternal repose of his soul, it crossed my mind that a few weeks before his death, one night I had a clear dream where I saw him inside the coffin. A cousin to whom I confided it the next day told me it meant exactly the opposite, that he was in the pink of health. Not to mention recurring dreams where I always see a body of water in the background, it may be a sea or a river with me wading in it but I never got drowned anyway. When I asked the rest of my siblings if they also had similar dreams, they answered in the negative. I then came to the conclusion that if among the six of us, his children, I was the only one who was not able to bid him good-bye personally because of immigration constraints here in the US at that time and which made it impossible for me to go home to the Philippines, yet I was the only one privileged to foresee his crossing over the threshold to the Great Beyond. At least, I was still blessed. I also realized that when my father first attempted to petition me shortly before he went home to the Philippines for good, he was required to submit a lot of credentials at so short a time that in the long run it was more practical for my mother to do it. She only had to attach a copy of my birth certificate to her application, which was subsequently approved by the immigration without much ado. Had my father done it, my petition would have died too upon his death.

The death of Dr. Domini in July of 1998 was the second blow for me. While still working for him in 1997, one morning he told me about a pain at the lumbar area of his body that had been bothering him now and then. I suggested that he see a doctor as soon as possible but I was not so sure if he took my unsolicited advice seriously because based from my experience with my husband, men, if possible, do not want medical attention unless they are probably in the brink of death. Anyway, his former secretary who called to inform me of his death following surgery from which he was not able to recover because of complications, told me his family had decided to take him off life support. He was plugged to it for two months.

Call it mental telepathy but that was in June when I had that nagging feeling of calling him up just to say, "Hello." Or was it him trying to get connected to me all the while that he was comatose?

"Lee leaves behind his mother, Rose; his children

(Andrew, James and Mary) and his grandchildren (Kim, Chris and Dave); and his dear friend, Mayette" thus read Dr. Domini's obituary in the newspaper, evoking a pang of nostalgia in me.

Unlike those salad days when I was still young and in quest for a deeper meaning of life to establish my self-identity, I guess I have reached the apex when I have mellowed because I do not want anymore to crystallize the "coincidences" in my life. It might direct me to see what is in store for me. I just want to have an open mind, let go, and have Somebody up there take the cudgel for me. Self-surrender, which was an anathema for me before, is now a thing of the past.

X

Temporal and Spiritual Prisms

It is said that for one who has faith, no explanation is needed but for one who does not have faith, no explanation is possible. To this teaser for one's imagination, I still could add that if one has faith and trust in the Divine Providence, His working in His own mysterious ways is fathomable because if He wants it done, He will always provide the means at His own time.

This I also found out in 1998.

I was then working as a housekeeper (a euphemistic term for a maid) after my brief stint with Shariff. I was curious as to how it is to be one here in the US so much so that when I saw an ad at the local newspaper for that position, I applied just for kicks and was accepted on the spot (my employer was obviously impressed on how a mere Filipino high school graduate, which I told her I am so as not to be overqualified for that position, could speak and write correct English). This position exposed me to how life is among the rich and famous, the lifestyle I discovered by way of comparison I don't long for and I don't mean

to be sour grapes. I still prefer that which is just simple
and uncomplicated; at least, you'd be free by then from the
fetters of anything or anyone.

Anyway, my employer this time was a soft-spoken
widow in her early 80s, the owner of a glass factory also
in Sacramento. She briefed me as to my job description:
for $1,000 a month, five days a week with Saturday and
Sunday as my free days while she herself stayed in her other
house (also with another housekeeper) in the affluent area
in San Francisco for her concerts and other cultural activities driving there in her Mercedes or Rolls Royce. I was
supposed to start my day at 7 AM Monday when I'd climb
the 15-winding steps going to her boudoir after picking up
the newspaper at the front door. Carrying her breakfast tray
consisting of hot tea concocted from special tea leaves and
a small piece of lightly buttered toast baked by a famous
pastry shop in the city, I would then get another tray (which
I thought at first was a wide footstool) hanging in the closet
(where her linens and sheets are stored after having been
laundered and ironed by a laundry company, this particular
amenity was not extended to me); place her breakfast tray
on top of it with the newspaper on the left side (per her
special instruction); open her door after a light knock; greet
her with "Good morning"; put the wider tray over her lap
for her discretionary action while watching TV in her bed
and make a disappearing act to attend to my other duties.

On Wednesdays, I had to check that the flowers all
over the house had been changed by Derek, that gay florist
whose service was free in exchange for accommodations in
my employer's cottage adjoining the main house. This he
shared with Tomas, the caretaker for ten years now who is

from Cuba and still awaiting for the final action of Immigration regarding his application for adjustment of his status
based on political asylum as a Castro escapee. Though with
separate quarters, they were always at each other's neck,
Tomas calling Derek "faggot" with the latter responding
"stupid idiot." The burden of rebuttal shifted from side to
side until one time that it reached such a degree that my
employer had to call the police to settle the dispute. Being
the lone rose between two sparring thorns in the domestic
front, they were gentlemen enough to give me proper cour-
tesies fearing that I might be a "snitch" and give them away,
Tomas for using the washing machine and dryer, which
were prohibited for him and Derek for bringing home every
night his male partner, a "no-no" for my employer, who did
not understand his sexual orientation.

I found out about her charitable involvement in the
community as attested by her various awards and plaques
of appreciation hanging in her library. She tried her best
to still maintain her looks (by going to the beauty parlor
once a week for her hair and nails) and figure by doing
twenty laps everyday in her heated indoor swimming pool
(the first time I saw one in a private residence and which I
was thankful for in my job) while listening to the piped-in
music (which I had turned on while she was getting ready
in her one-piece brand-name bathing suit). Meantime that
I was dusting off her plants (to check for aphids) that adorn
the area (her decorator's professional fee was not peanuts)
and keeping an eye on her, this last assignment her dog,
Kirmet, and I had in common. Later on, when she went
back to her room with her canine companion to change
in the same way that they came down, that is, by way of a

private elevator with direct access to her private quarters, it was still my job to open the roof of the swimming pool by remote control to let off the steam.

All these I did for a month and a half in my required white uniform with matching shoes provided by my employer herself, marking the chasm that separates the mistress of the place from a lowly servant.

Such a scenario made me think about could there be a lot of homeless people in this rich country when there are only the two of us living in this two-level twenty-room house (with a five-car garage), which I sometimes find spooky I imagine myself to be Nancy Drew (my favorite teenage sleuth when I was in the elementary grades) about to discover some secrets in the closets; or where we could communicate only by intercom when she's up there and I'm down here; a sophisticated alarm system installed to assure us that we'd still be alive and kicking the next day; Kirmet's visit to his veterinarian for his regular "pedicure" (I did not know dogs get one until then) could already feed a family of seven for a fortnight in a third world country; in this nation where a reward for a lost mongrel is more than that for a lost child, it would not be a surprise to have Kirmet's name included in my employer's will instead of the name of a charitable institution and considering how close my employer was to Kirmet (he sleeps in his own couch in her own room, his particular dog scent pleasant to her olfactory sense), I'm sure during her wake when Kirmet outlives her, there will be a be-ribboned "From Kirmet with Love" wreath at the foot of her bier.

But that is not the crux of the matter yet.

One time while taking a shower in my own bathroom, I discovered a lump as big as a hen's egg in my right breast. I got the scare of my life considering the implication and the fact that I did not have health insurance of any kind. I still can't understand it but "something" hit me right in the head: an inspiration to ask the Blessed Virgin for help. I started immediately my nine-day miraculous medal novena with that particular petition in mind.

Two days after while fixing my room, I heard on the radio an announcement which came between a commercial break about this program of the state regarding a free mammogram for women 40 and over who qualify. In a jiffy I called up the 1-800 number, was interviewed over the phone, and assured of a free packet to arrive at my given address within the next three days. Following instructions, I requested Sophie to drive me to the local hospital of my choice in Sacramento for a physical examination; had a mammogram; then an ultrasound (and I thought it was only for pre-natal services), and finally a fine needle aspiration done by a pathologist all these medical services in less than a month for free, and to top it all, that notorious lump was just a simple cyst.

Another notable addendum in my favor was a free extended ob-gyne assistance with my soft-spoken lady doctor who shocked me during our first encounter when she asked me, "Are you sexually active?" to which I answered, "Oh, no, Doctor. That's rather unthinkable, because although far from my husband, I believe and practise chastity by choice. I put much premium on my moral life, you know". My sister nurse told me later on that is one of the basic diagnostic queries always asked here in the US. Well, what may be a wild guess to one could evoke a flabbergasting reaction to another specially if the latter is not used to it.

XI

First Test of Faith

It is an accepted truism that nothing is more permanent than change and that in life there are no guarantees, including human relationship. What may be true today may not be the same tomorrow, so it is best to take life as it comes with an open attitude, "play it by ear," as they say.

While in Sacramento, Sophie used to tell me that I was a "rolling stone" and I would rebut, "Perhaps, but one that gathers moss." At some points in one's life, priorities change. What before was foremost in my hierarchy of needs was adjustment of my status although it meant working in a job with low pay. Now, it's for financial break.

I told myself I had enough of long-range planning for an unproductive venture and that what is important at this point in my life is the "HERE" and "NOW." I want to have much so that I can share it with more, not only my family in Manila and never mind the issue of adjusting my status which, if really is for me, will be worked out eventually in my favor without me raking through my gray matter as to the "how."

A better job offer with a lot of perks in San Francisco in February of 1999 made me decide to relocate. I was to work as a companion to a very nice Italian lady, Alice, in her early 90s and still ambulatory, living in a plush area at the Sunset district. Actually, it was a holdover from my cousin-in-law, Bertha, who was referred to that job by a former co-teacher. Both had been under my father's supervision when he was still their school principal in the Philippines and I was sure, he was never a mean boss to his subordinates so I was a bit disappointed on how she could have gone down so low to have lost her sense of decency when she charged Bertha and me the equivalent of our two-day pay instead of just waiting for us to give her a gift as a token of our appreciation for helping us get that job.

I paid the bill and that made us on equal footing. Anyway, Bertha was going home to the Philippines, having finished her allowable six-month stay here as authorized by Immigration but before she left, she explicitly told me (she called me up at Sacramento advising me to leave my $80 per night job there to take over her place) she would just look for another job the moment she comes back after an indefinite time. Also, the fact that I have two sisters (both registered nurses) and their families in the city who I thought could provide a strong support system for me was another factor I took into consideration for my relocation to the Bay Area.

Without much fanfare, I was at this time involved with some of my personal charitable projects in the Philippines, the recipients of whom are my mother and her helper; an unwed mother of three sickly children, and an orphanage (mostly disabled children) run by a congregation of nuns (with special request that I be noted as an anonymous benefactress just like what I do when I give my donations. "What your right hand does, don't let your left hand see it"). Sometimes when asked why despite my financial instability here in America, I still "bother" to "give away" what meager earnings I manage to have instead of keeping it all for myself and my family, I just smile and shrug. Why should I bother to explain to one who can't understand the reasons for my action? After all, it is not the question of how much income one has but his desire to share whatever he has. We still have to hear of a Lotto jackpot winner announcing to give even a fraction of his prize to charity. And isn't it a $64 question if you'd try to understand why some people consider it "sky is the limit" for their splurges and other worldly pursuits when but a $5-donation is already a big deal for them.

When I know I am interacting with somebody who "travels on the same wavelength as I" (for doesn't "water seek its own level"?), I would give an answer that I hope will reinforce his resolution to also serve best the "Big Boss" up there. I believe that life is the greatest gift God gave us and we can make it more meaningful if we share with our least brethren whatever blessings in any form we have received from Him. This is in conjunction with sharing your potentials and time wisely in His service which could serve as our greatest gift to Him. When I die, at least, I can tell Him what I did for Him with love when I was still here on earth which is the very first question He'll ask all His subjects when they meet Him for the first time aside from taking seriously the "Principle of Holy Law," which says, "Human action now will be met by a corresponding action of God at the final judgment."

On the other hand, I also have learned that right here on earth we can already experience the truth of "whatever you sow, you reap" and sometimes you'd even reap double what you sowed, just like in 1995, when after mailing a $25-check to the "Food for the Poor," which was against the advice of a cousin of mine (who won't even dole out her junk and who told me my benevolence was impractical inasmuch as I was still in that "hit-and-run" stage here in the US) a week after I received a $50 birthday cash gift from Dr. Domini.

Anyway, everything was running smoothly, or so I thought, with Alice and myself bonding with each other when in June Bertha called up from the Philippines, telling me she is coming back in August and could I possibly look for a room we could both rent and stay in during our off days. I then called up a dear friend, Michelle, a department chair and highly respected teacher at an exclusive Catholic school in the city who in turn referred me to a mother of one of their students. If our primary objective did not materialize, I was thankful I was led to her because she must have been instrumental in my new apostolate of being a volunteer at a soup kitchen serving the city's homeless, another eye-opener for me from which I would learn more of life's realities here in the land of Uncle Sam.

My first "test of faith" came in August.

When Bertha came back from the Philippines, she requested me to give her two days of my six-day job even insinuating that my reliever be "kicked out" to give way to her but I refused.

"That's not fair," I told her. But I assured her that I'd negotiate her request with Alice's daughter who would be the one to decide of our internal arrangement. I was even willing to sacrifice my two-day salary just to help her out financially, even reminding her that I was against her going home hastily last February because it might be difficult for her to look for another job considering her legal status when she comes back.

I was damn right.

"But I did not leave you that job!" was what she responded which surprised me because that was not what we had agreed upon in the first place. Then I remembered that she had a track record way back home of being a pathological liar (she could lie without batting an eyelash) with me as the unsuspecting victim of her devious design this time.

"No! I don't want any changes!" Alice's daughter was visibly outraged when I presented to her Bertha's proposal. That was the first time I saw her get mad because I knew her to be sweet-tempered and soft-spoken until then.

When I told Bertha about it later, I received a cool response from her. I never had an idea what she was up to until I received a call from Alice's daughter.

"Bertha called me up a while ago and she was begging back her job but I told her she'd been away for so long I can't reconsider her request. Please tell her not to call me up again".

My goodness me, how I had to apologize to my client's daughter for a faux pas not of my own doing. But I learned another moral lesson here: an action done in bad faith because of a selfish motive will never prosper and as long as my conscience is clear before Him up there, I don't give a damn if Bertha's husband who condoned what his wife did, has the impression that I am Madam Machiavelli, which I am not.

I also discerned that Mama Mary in her maternal goodness will always guide and protect me wherever I go; otherwise, how could you explain her picture (as the "Lady of Sorrows") on top of my bed's headboard, the very first thing that caught my attention when I first came into my room to start work with Alice?

XII

Second Test of Faith - The Balloon Bursts

My second "test of faith" was in 2000, the scenario and the protagonists involved I never expected even in my wildest dreams but that is because life is full of surprises.

Although I was already working full-time with Alice in San Francisco, I had to go back to Sacramento now and then for my subsequent medical check-up. Most of the time, I'd spend the night at Sophie's carehome and her staff would divulge to me some of their domestic problems, which I understood were inevitable in any organizational set-up where communication breakdowns sometimes occur. Trying to be a peacemaker to diffuse the tension, I would then advise them to be frank and honest with Sophie for a smooth working relationship.

Yolie, Sophie's niece and one of her caregivers, took me into her confidence one time that I was there. She is married with her husband and five children still in the Philippines.

"Please help me find a job in San Francisco. I'm so over-worked here with just a meager salary I can hardly send something home," she said to me. She was just getting $1,000 a month, no fixed days as "off" depending on Sophie's discretion and with six clients to take care of, one who needs lifting weighing 200 pounds. That was the very same reason before why I did not accept Sophie's offer to work for her.

"Working in a carehome where you are supposed to take care of six residents is far different from working on a one-on-one basis, salary-wise included. Why don't you be honest and tell Sophie about your plans to relocate for a change? Also, I think it would be fair to her if you'd wait for your replacement first before making the move," I told her, trying to be of help. She followed up her request by calling me up for several nights afterwards when Sophie and Gerry went home to their residence.

"Yolie wants to look for a job there in San Francisco. Would you be kind enough to help her?" Sophie called me up two weeks after my encounter with Yolie.

"She told me about her plan to relocate here but I advised her not to leave unless she has somebody to take over her place in your carehome," I was thankful that she was open to Yolie's plan, or so I thought.

"Oh, it's all right.I'm sure we can more than manage. I've also called up a friend of mine in Oroville to see if she can accommodate her," she assured me.

"I don't have a one-day reliever here at the moment. If she wants, she can have it while she is looking for a full-time job," I said.

"That would be fine," she assured me before hanging up. Later on, Yolie told me she heard this conversation between Sophie and me while they were preparing dinner that night. Naive as I was, I never suspected Yolie's real motive in moving to San Francisco staying with her friends. Per our agreement and Sophie's full knowledge, she came to relieve me at 10 Saturday morning and checked out at 10 also in the morning of the following day although I had to be with Alice at night who looked forward to my return on the same day what with our bonding for quite some time. One time when I came back after spending the night with one of my sisters, Yolie told me Alice wanted to call the police for fear that I might have met an accident - hence, I was not able to come home. She was already in the early stage of Alzheimer's disease she must have forgotten that I even called her up from my sister's place to check upon them.

It was on the third Saturday that Yolie spilled the beans. She was really after an 80-year-old disabled widower who had courted and proposed marriage to her while he was still one of the residents at Sophie's neighbor's carehome also in Sacramento. He had been transferred here to San Francisco. Looking upon him as the means to justify her end where getting his citizenship is concerned for adjustment of her status, she decided to gamble on this option. After all, she and her husband had already made a feasibility study of what she would do even before she left for the US: get a "quickie" divorce in Reno; marry her "knight" in a wheelchair sans his shining armor; petition her kids in the Philippines; and bingo, they would live happily ever after in the land of milk and honey.

"But that is just like selling your soul to the highest bidder," I reminded her when she admitted it was not a marriage of convenience she had in mind but the real McCoy.

"It's okay. Anyway, I'm sure God will understand," she said in justification of her lack of moral scruples.

Oh, well, I thought, it is true God's plan is for us to be with Him in heaven but if you want otherwise, He will respect your free will, our freedom of choice just like what He did to Adam and Eve at the garden of Eden.

She also confided that she told her folks at Sacramento about her relieving me for two days instead of our 24-hour agreement to save her pride and not appear pitiful to them.

"Don't worry. It's no big deal," she assured me.

However, the "no big deal" later on turned out to be a great fiasco because Sophie denied she ever requested me to help Yolie relocate to San Francisco and even branded me an "ungrateful wretch" because I "pirated" Yolie from her working force when I knew she was short of staff, not to mention cheating Yolie who, she said, relieved me here for two days but was paid only for one day of work. To all these allegations, Yolie decided to keep mum instead of setting the records straight because she maintained she was indebted to Sophie and couldn't bear to put her down.

"See what you got from being a 'Good Samaritan'," one of my sisters taunted me when she learned of the tight fix I was in.

"Face your own music your own way," added my other sibling.

Doesn't it hurt you most when you realize that having come from the same womb is not a guarantee that you would stick together through thick and thin if one's personal interest is at stake? But then, even Christ himself was abandoned by those who claimed to be His friends when worse came to worst.

An update on Yolie: her Reno marriage flopped after barely five months. When the honeymoon was over; she went back to Sophie and Gerry, the former with a gleaming "I-told-you-so" look on her face and it was back to square one for Yolie. At least, "birds of a feather flock together." Lately, I learned that her "convenient" husband died and her petition for adjustment of her status was shelved into her lawyer's dead file, the equivalent of a newsroom's morgue.

Sometimes, she'd call me up to tell me of her latest kaleidoscopic episode but I always check my compassionate nature, reminding myself that I had done enough for her. At least, I did not commit the sin of ommission but even became the scapegoat of somebody's whims and caprices One could forgive but things won't be the same again.

In the course of one's introspection, he'd find out that it would be beyond human endurance to assume the role of "Atlas." It is impossibile to carry on one's shoulders all the cares of the world. A messianic complex? And that if one wants to maintain his equilibrium, sometimes it is best to be cocooned in one's microcosm be a pragmatist but with his heart and mind still directed to Somebody up there. After all, at the end of our life, it will be an individual accounting between you and Him, right?

But on the second thought, my latest "test of faith" must have been more of a boon, not much of a bane, a "blessing in disguise" because it enabled me to discover another facet of life's stark reality: how one could find a strong support system during his emotional and spiritual aridity from people not necessarily related to him by consanguinity or affinity but could bond with him in their quest for truth. It must be a tough struggle to attempt to be close to a person when your values are on different dimensions unless a compromise could be worked out. By then, you might disprove that "too much familiarity breeds contempt" because you already have reached that point when "you can look at the same thing in the same way."

XIII

On Role Models

When I was growing up in the Philippines, I had role models who were dynamic rather than static, depending on the biological age I was in. I cannot remember fully well if I had one in the elementary grades where my love for books started although it was exactly the opposite with any lesson in math, my Achilles heel. In high school, I had two: "Sir Toting," who taught us Algebra with a wonderful sense of humor that lessened my apathy to the subject and "Sir Supe," who enhanced my interest in world history. We had then mischievously branded our teachers behind their backs and beyond their hearing distance.

At a prestigious Catholic university in Iloilo City, also in the Philippines, where I finished my bachelor's degree in 1970, I never wanted to miss my class in Theatre Arts with Mr. Rolando Agnas, who used to humble himself telling us that his face was one that only a mother could love (I remembered how one of my classmates commented he looked like a cherub who has grown up) and teased our imagination with his "one should be consistently consistent in his consistency," or when one says,"No, I don't love you," it means that she does because two like signs ("No" and "don't love") equals one positive sign ("I love you"). I also admired the professionalism of Mr. Rodolfo Claparols, who taught us the six Ws (what, who, when, where, why, and how) in our News Journalism class. Likewise, I still retain the discipline of "keeping one's cool under fire" or grace under pressure I learned from my Argumentation and Debate class under Atty. Luis Tirol, a top-seeded tennis player and every inch a gentleman who sent our teenage hearts fluttering.

That was the time when I was attracted to my mentors who fed my intellectual insatiability.

Then, when I was a public information officer at a government office in Iloilo City for nine months way back in 1975, I had high respects for Atty. Concepcion Amamanglon who penned her labor dispute decisions with great honesty and credibility.

The latest addition to my roster of role models was Luzvimin Deano whom I affectionately called "Manang Luz" ("manang" is an address showing respect for someone older than you in the Filipino context). Our mothers used to be best friends here in San Francisco. I visualized it when she told me how when our fathers were still alive, they would play barber to each other to save the bother and budget of going to the barber's shop. An active charismatic leader and deep into the healing ministry, Manang Luz was one person who lived the Gospel through her actions though some people see them as bordering spiritual fanaticism. Choosing to rather live a spartan way of life, she also deserved commendation for sacrificing what was supposed to be alloted for her basic needs so as to be able to send it to her relatives way back home who are asking for financial help as well as the monthly donation envelopes that come for different charitable causes, a clear illustration of sharing until it hurts, not sharing only if you have some surplus.

Manang Luz could exemplify a Christian daughter who takes the third commandment of "honor thy father and mother" on a deeper degree, a rarity here in America when you could call your parents by their first names. She aptly combined career and parental duties and obligation on the same level to the point of forgetting herself most of the time. This attitude of sacrificing one's needs and interests for one's parents is inherent in the Filipino culture, where one could usually find the eldest daughter who had been oriented to forego marriage or entering the convent to take care of her aged parents or younger siblings. It is hard to decipher where the bottleneck is and why, when you come across situations that don't reflect this particular cultural heritage - just like a Filipino neighbor, a chemist working in a laboratory here in the city and earning four times an hour what a housekeeper or caregiver does but abhors the idea of sending a mere pittance of $50 a month to his mother in the Philippines, maintaining it is too much for his budget, or a Filipino resident I befriended in a long-term care facility where I volunteer every Sunday whose five children just living here in San Francisco and Daly City are too busy to visit him on weekends.

"But this is already America!" I remembered my aunt telling me one time when we were analyzing the metamorphosis some of our countrymen undergo upon relocation in their adopted country.

In a society characterized by crass materialism where emphasis is on the epicurean philosophy of "live today for tomorrow you die" or what somebody told me, "I don't care if I die tonight as long as I had enjoyed life," and where God is sometimes considered irrelevant for some with spiritual enrichment misconstrued as a quest for pseudotranscendentalism, role models serving as paragon of virtues are endangered species.

Postscript:

Manang Luz died March 10, 2003 after a seven month fight with cancer.

Dropping by their house three days after her burial, I witnessed some extraordinary manifestations which, according to her mother and her sister, happened for the first time. When I passed in front of their heater, it turned on by itself, with a loud sound audible enough to be heard by the three of us. At the same time, I noticed a very bright yellow light emanating from it and a strong gust of warm air directly blowing at me.

To my probing questions later on, I found out that the heater is not automatic. It could be turned on without a sound, with the pilot light simply flickering at its bottom. Then the heat escapes gradually from the vent.

Was that Manang Luz sending us a message from the Great Beyond? Was she telling us that we should instead be happy at her passing because death is just like coming home? After all, she had spent her entire life here on earth serving the Lord.

Whatever it was, we welcome it with an open mind.

XIV

Agape at the Blue Acres

One of the two humanitarian and spiritual exposures I enjoyed most during my stay in the US was my volunteer work at The Blue Acres, a 1,100-bed-capacity long-term care facility known as an almshouse, a hospice for the elderly and handicapped poor. For two centuries now, the complex has been situated on top of one of the rolling hills outside Millbrae, a city outside San Francisco.

I started my involvement there in October 2000 having learned about their needs from *The Catholic San Francisco*, an official newspaper of the Archdiocese of San Francisco. Never did I have an inkling of my parents having volunteered there, too, when they were still here in the US, not until three months after I started mine when my mother told me how my father loved and enjoyed his apostolate there. Was it he who again guided me?

Anyway, on Sundays, deciding not to take the shuttle bus which regularly takes passengers to and from the hospital, I would trudge my way up on the snaking path, hitting two birds with one stone, to enable me to exercise my legs and to lose some few pounds in the process with my wanting it at the same time that I admire the wonderful panorama before my eyes specially when the sun comes out in all its glory, the verdant hills around punctuated by houses and buildings of various architectural designs showing man's ingenuity against the backdrop of nature, a thought-provoking combination. And as I feel in my lungs bursts of energy from breathing the freshness of the morning dew and the visible mist that I exhale afterwards, the cycle seems to be an allegorical representation of how God's graces are bestowed on us though undiscernibly by the human eyes but take visible form as a consequence of how we deal with it.

The Catholic mass starts at 10:15 AM but a couple of hours before that volunteers acting as chapel escorts fetch the residents in their wheelchairs from their rooms to bring them down to the chapel on the first floor. The whole activity shows a beautiful symbiotic relationship between the Benefactor and His beneficiaries, the former working on the volunteers who come from all walks of life; of cultural diversity with different eccentricities doing the ministry for as long as thirty years and never mind whatever their hidden agendum is (whether it is for the Lord or self-serving); not subject to gender or age profiling and other what-have-you's. At the receiving end are the elderly and the handicapped (physically and mentally) who are at The Blue Acres either by choice or neccesity. They all have as a common denominator how much a visit from a relative or friend can assuage their longing for human contact. That must be the feeling of that elderly Chinese lady I see every Sunday in the hallway of the fourth floor whose enjoyment at the company of her son is very visible in her face (an "ambush" interview with him revealed she could not remember anybody anymore because of a stroke) as he feeds her with the food he has brought her at the same time that he banters with her, his regular Sunday schedule without fail for two years now although he still comes from Oakland which is a good 30-minute drive away.

The one-hour mass is celebrated by the chaplain of the facility with logistical support from the volunteers themselves acting as servers, eucharistic ministers, lectors, and choir members. Likewise, the residents themselves with the volunteers coaching them to bring the offerings to the altar. As the recessional hymn is sung by the choir who sometimes sings a capella if Steve, the gifted pianist, is not around, everybody feels energized with one's spiritual batteries recharged and the physical side catered to afterwards during the fellowship that follows suit, a gesture of thanks and appreciation from the hospital.

- ALAN -

It was in this extraordinary atmosphere showing agape or Christian love that I came to know Alan, who would not have caught anybody's fancy had he been just a regular guy doing his regular apostolate on a regular Sunday at The Blue Acres.

An only child with a rather boyish look true of his German-Irish descent, he might just be another face in the maddening crowd out there at San Francisco's financial district but what makes him stand out from among the rest and which impressed me most is the fact that he could serve as chapel escort, lector, eucharistic minister, and counsellor all rolled into one in his prosthetic arms and legs and always in a short-sleeved shirt without much qualm, the type you don't meet everyday of your life. But that is just the "tip of the iceberg" for I found out that he is more substantial than I first thought he was when I was observing him in his unguarded moments. He later told me he did not mind being the subject of my scrutiny, observing people being one of my rather unconventional hobbies because it makes my mind work.

"It has always been inherent in me to want to help other people," he revealed to me during our informal interaction (the usual tete-a-tete I like doing with my characters) where he was kind enough to accommodate me upon my request. That was after he came back from his weekend recollection at Burlingame. "It is one activity where I find fulfillment, my disability being a plus factor for me in reaching out to people in the same boat because I can empathize with them much better than if I were just a regular guy."

Just 37, Alan finished his MA in Counseling and has been working as a counselor for nine years now. His job description calls for working with students with physical disabilities, networking with them in and out of the school campus.

Aside from his Sunday commitment at The Blue Acres, Alan heads the local team of a Christian organization that provides a support system to people who have lost their spouses either by divorce or death. They put up retreats on two weekends twice a year.

"Open to love": that is how he plans his future. His

divorce is not a hindrance for his moving on to a brighter tomorrow beyond the perimeter of his disability.

- NENE -

"But I just sing in the bathroom" was what I kiddingly answered "Nene" (which means "little girl" in Filipino) when she .asked me to join them at the choir. Never in my life had I joined a choir or any musical group before, public speaking and literary writing my cup of tea during my salad days in college and later on, taking charge of office communications, my area of responsibility in my professional life. It is true during the Sunday masses in Manila I attended regularly with my family, I sang praises to the Lord from my heart but with the rest of the congregation.

However, when I later on observed that there was only a handful of volunteers in the choir, I decided to help putting into practise what little ear for music I have (I play the piano, all right, but not as well as my daughter, MC, who had been at the conservatory of music of Sta. Isabel College in Manila for eight years under the patient tutelage of Miss Lenela Ledesma for her piano lessons and she could sing, too, having won several medals and trophies in several singing competitions also in Manila – her talent must be the result of listening to the music from the little radio I used to put next to her ear in her crib when she was just a baby) and telling myself that if God wants you to serve Him in any way He wants it, He is going to bring out the best of you but with your consent, of course, never forcing anybody.

Anyway, the main reason why I decided to include Nene as one of my true-to-life characters in this memoir just like the rest was an extraordinary thing that happened to her one Sunday in October 2001. Both of us were actually taking the third flight of steps on our way down to the bus stop, the usual route we take after the mass and our fellowship. I was dragging her bag on wheels (which I usually do to help her with her burden) and we were on the thirteenth step going down when suddenly I saw her roll down just like a big bundle preceded by the cane she always carries to support herself. My initial reaction was to reach out to her but to no avail because there was a three-feet-high-double-tiered-iron-railing between us preventing me from going over to her side. Running down with my adrenaline working in full gear with her bag still in tow, I was on time to lessen the impact as her body fell on the last step. Answering me in the affirmative when I asked her if she was okay, I was relieved when I checked and found that she did not have any life-threatening fractures. Suddenly, a van passed by and stopped when I waved my hands to catch their attention. Inside were some of our co-volunteers who for some reason had been kept from leaving the premises earlier, which was unusual for them. The "Good Samaritans" drove Nene home.

"Was that your hand trying to catch me as I fell down the steps last Sunday?" Nene greeted me good-naturedly that next Sunday. I had all but forgotten the previous incident what with other priorities that kept my mind busy.

"No, I couldn't even reach you from where I was, considering that railing between us, remember?" I answered nonchalantly.

Then, she narrated the facts: as she was rolling down the steps one by one, she saw a smooth arm (up to the elbow) from out of what seemed to be clouds trying to catch her and she tried her best to grab it.

In retrospect, several questions kept on nagging me: were my co-volunteers delayed as a mere coincidence or was it deliberately caused for a reason? They came when they were needed most. Whose arm was trying to catch her as she fell thirteen steps down, then, coming out unscathed considering her age and physical condition?

She also had mentioned about the medal of St. Francis of Assisi pinned inside the vest she was wearing that day. It had been given to her by a friend telling her that it would help her in time of distress.

Or, was it Psalm 91 (Security under God's Protection) in action?

In private life, Nene was born in Manila 72 summers ago. She came to the US at 27 when she married a Filipino naturalized US citizen 28 years her senior with whom she has three children. Her initial involvement as a volunteer started at The Blue Acres where her late husband was a resident for eight years and continued even after his death until now, a good 23 years later, rain or shine. What she lacks in height, she more than makes it up in serving the Lord starting at 6:30 AM every Sunday when she acts as chapel escort interacting with the residents on a one-on-one basis; choir member; rosary leader; and eucharistic minister (she also does this ministry at her parish church). She maintains that her ambition to be a nurse and a nun she found in her apostolate at the facility.

On the practical side of life, Nene has been a well-liked

teacher's aide at an elementary school at San Francisco for thirty-two years now where her job description calls for helping children improve their reading skills and overall classroom management.

- JERRY -

" 'Jerry' with a 'J' " - that's what I used to call my "partner in sanctity" affectionately.

" 'Meriam' with an 'E' " he would answer me.

If there is one thing that I never could forget about Jerry, it is how he reminds me of my late father in many ways: the way he walks with a little stoop and a hurried gait; a ready and sincere smile for everyone he meets at The Blue Acres; every inch a gentleman and a supportive man who always makes me feel I'm my father's little girl again (when I told him I'm scared of needles, he assured me he'd be there to hold my hands when I'd undergo our annual TB test). I even suspected that it was my dear father who must have led me to him or vice-versa; otherwise, how could one justify the coincidences when our paths always crossed each other without us planning it. We were classmates in our orientation class in October 2000; we joined the lectors' group at the same time; both of us were supposed to be sent to the School of Pastoral Leadership classes for our care ministry certificate for the sacrament of healing and eucharistic ministry to the homebound; we are both chapel escorts and sometimes troubleshoot as elevator operators. But there is one item in his job description that is not included in mine: everybody appreciates it when he brings down our food cart from the hospital kitchen every Sunday for our fellowship because by then we can be assured all items are complete, thanks to his meticulous attention.

Jerry at 73 is a professional artist who does portraits, seascapes, and still lifes in oil. He discovered his gift when he was ten, turning professional at fifty-five after having seen every nook of the world as a merchant marine at 16 (and for the next twelve years of his life) and later on honed under the tutelage of professionals in the field.

"But I was a barber first before being a professional artist to be able to live and raise my family," he humbly asserted but such occupation must have motivated his three daughters to follow his footsteps. They have consequently established their own niche in the hair science business and are now successful hairdressers themselves.

Before his involvement at The Blue Acres, Jerry used to volunteer in driving cancer patients from their home to the hospital and back with the same enthusiasm he exuded in serving the homeless as a cook at the soup kitchen at the St. Vincent de Paul. All these altruistic activities are with the encouragement and support of his charming Greek Orthodox wife of forty-eight years, Chula, who he considers the greatest blessing in his life.

"What I'm giving back to God is just an iota of what I received from Him because He gave me so much" is his rationale as to why he is so active in the Lord's vineyard.

Remember the parable of the talents?

- INENG -

The first time I met Ineng was when we volunteers were taking back the residents to their rooms after the mass. She

was beaming with that smile which was as sincere as her
"hello," making her look younger than her sixty years, augmented by her warm personality. That day marked the start
of our friendship.

" 'Ineng' which means 'small girl' in Marinduque (an
island in the Philippines, famous for its Moriones festival,
a tourist attracttion) was my father's pet name for me," she
said when I asked her preferred name she would want to
be used in my book. Just like me, she was also close to
her father when she was still a kid and would follow him
around.

Consistently on top of her class in the elementary grades,
her desire for further academic pursuit was hindered by the
absence of a high school in their area, the usual scenario
during her time. So much so that at the tender age of 17,
she sailed for Manila in search of a greener pasture landing
a job as a domestic helper for six employers for the next
forty years of her life.

"It was for the sake of my two kids, to give them a
better future that I decided to stay put here in the US for
twenty years now," she confided to me. She was referring to
her two daughters (she is not married to their father), now
24 and 23 who she last saw in 1982 when she came home to
the Philippines, after her first trip around the world with
her last employers.

Then in 1983 after their second trip abroad following
the same itinerary which the rich and famous normally
take, they decided to leave her (but with her consent) at
their plush home in Portola, CA, to work as housekeeper
for their guests and business associates from Asian coun-

tries. They themselves would just come to the US twice a year sending her monthly salary on a regular basis.

In 1990 when most of her friends (she was a "fairy godmother" to them helping them in her own way) were working on their papers with Immigration for adjustment of their status, her employers suggested that she follow suit but offering all sort of excuses did not give her back her passport which all the time was at their safekeeping. It was only in 1996 when they eventually handed it to her; by then, it was too late for her claim had already become moot and academic. It was also at this time that her employers decided to start withholding her salary as her nest egg with them, promising to give it to her when and if she would need it in the near future. No public instrument was signed to this effect by both parties, Ineng acting in good faith and trusting on their word of honor.

Ineng had to leave the services of her sixth employers last 1999 when they sold their house in Portola. She was not given any cash bonus as should be the customary token of an employer in appreciation for the loyalty and job well done by the employee. Broke, it was back to square one for her.

Always for the underdog, I could not help but admire her faith in God and perseverance to still go on of a marginalized entity after such life's bitter trials. Her green card, S18,000 in back wages, and the maternal instinct of a mother to hug her two daughters - all these remain her elusive dreams up to this writing.

- MIMI -

"I was a lost sheep!" That was the statement, which I noticed had a tinge of bitterness, Mimi blurted out one morning while we were having coffee and doughnuts during our fellowship. We had just brought back the residents to their rooms after the 10:15 AM mass. The subsequent activity always gives us volunteers time to exchange pleasantries after doing our job as chapel escorts, lectors, eucharistic ministers and choir members here at The Blue Acres.

"Oh, really." I was taken aback by her revealation.

"I did not even know Jesus Christ until 1990." That coup de grace further made me curious as to the "why" behind her allegation. We were not so close then; our acquaintanceship limited only to our Sunday interaction but whether or not she was inspired by the Holy Spirit that day so as to trust me (she never had an idea that I was in the writing business before and I had told myself five years ago I had enough of it) with her life story which, she said, she wanted to share (she confided that five years ago, she prayed for somebody to write her biography because of the moral lesson in it) to touch other people's lives, I was thankful that she did it (an "assignment"?).

Mimi was a product of a broken home. She and five other siblings grew up in the care of her maternal grandparents who provided them their basic physical needs but nothing that catered to the emotional and spiritual levels.

For the first thirty years of her life, she had entered the church twice only: for her baptism and consequently her confirmation which in her native country was compulsory for children at the age of five. At the tender age of ten, she was almost raped by the three closest male members of her family. All these traumatic experiences as a child, aggravated later on during her adult life by a convenient and loveless marriage that eventually led to an inevitable separation, left her indelible marks making her incorrigibly cynical to the "goodness of the Lord".

During a pleasure trip to the Vatican in 1981, she bought three miniature statues of the Infant Jesus of Prague intending to send two of them by mail to her mother in the Philippines, but was quite hesitant thinking they were so fragile they might break into pieces on the way. When she had them blessed upon her return to the US, the priest who did it mentioned casually about a fellow priest living with them at that time and bound for the Philippines in a couple of days. Of course he would be more than willing to bring the statues to her mom, which he did.

Yet such "coincidence" did not stir something in her, spiritual or otherwise.

"I was in the 'dark tunnel' for forty-one years," she told me, " until I befriended a contemplative nun who nagged me into going to a serious confession, my very first, which I tried to put off for a while. After I told her on the phone that I had decided to make it, until now I can't simply explain it but it seemed that like St. Paul on the road to Damascus, my eyes were opened for the first time and I felt elated!" The next day, she went to confession and for the very first time in her life cried so much, both for feeling sorry for all her past sins and vowing to start a new life in the Lord's embrace that she still is euphoric.

She was not just "a" lost sheep, but rather "the" lost sheep, so special He left the 99 to look patiently for her and how happy He was to find her.

He successfully brought her home.

- EVELYN AND BOBBY -

"Of course, I'd be honored to be one of the characters in your book but with Bobby, too," was the deal Evelyn, a resident at The Blue Acres for five years, struck with me without much ado. "He's my angel," was her addendum.

"No problem," I answered, feeling excited, my sixth sense telling me that here I have a scoop. I could remember what our professor in journalism way back in college used to remind us to always "nose" for "news": "news" being "if a dog bites a man, it isn't news; but if a man bites a dog, then it is news."

Evelyn and Bobby as a lovey-dovey couple could raise eyebrows and make one's gray matter work when they sit and sing with us in the choir every Sunday. Such initial perception is quite justifiable if one bases his impression on what he sees physically but not to one who understands that "there is more than what meets the eye" considering the conspicuous opposite attributes each one possesses. Black, Evelyn, who is wheelchair bound at 62, has been totally blind for three years now (an aftermath for diabetes of which she undergoes dialysis three times a week) is a smart lady with a quick mind; and has a distinct beauty of her own (beauty being subjective). White, Bobby at 77, walks with a stocky gait in his suspenders and exudes that kind and charming aura in his face while acting as Evelyn's chapel escort. She came to the East Coast in 1962 from Punta Gorda (part of Guatemala) before settling down here at California in 1988; got her training as a CNA (certified nursing assistant) here at The Blue Acres in 1989 and worked as a home health aide from 1989-1993. He came in 1964 with his brother, Richard, from Chicago and they have been staying in Cadillac Hotel here at San Francisco ever since. As an auxiliary member of the Legion of Mary at the facility, her apostolate is spreading devotion to the rosary by initiating the daily rosary in her ward - a tangible proof showing that a physical disability need not be a barrier in serving the Lord. Bobby, on the other hand, is not much of a churchgoer unless he is with Evelyn.

They met in 1988 inasmuch as they were staying in the same hotel building but their association did not go beyond the casual "hi" and "hello" until 1994, when Evelyn broke her knee one night from a fall when she was walking home from work. It was at 8 AM one day that year when somebody told Bobby (he was working as a cook in that hotel that time) a lady staying at Rm. 238 (Evelyn's) wanted him to bring her coffee. He did as requested and that was their first encounter of the close kind.

"I remembered him to be good-natured and kind," she told me when I asked her how come, of all people, she thought of Bobby in particular to do the favor.

The next day, Evelyn prayed that Bobby would again bring her coffee. Suddenly, out of the blue and without much preamble, he appeared in her door with the steaming coffee for her, which idea, he said, just flashed into his mind. That was their second encounter of the close kind.

"I know you have been praying for me to come with your coffee, so here it is," was Bobby's greeting when he showed up for the third time at Evelyn's unit.

The rest is history.

When the three of us sat down in the hallway of the fifth floor of The Blue Acres for our bull session, I made it clear to them (just like what I usually do to my interviewees) that if they do not want to answer any of my questions because it might be an intrusion into their privacy, by all means I'd respect it. This was what I was expecting from them, to clam up when I brought up the issue of "relationship" between the two of them but I got a rather positive reaction.

"I love Evelyn but I told her from the very start that she cannot expect a serious commitment from me because I'm married to my mother and brother, aside from the fact that I am divorced with a daughter in the East Coast, although I have lost contact with them," Bobby explained matter-of-factly.

"I also told him I cannot entertain any relationship with him more than friendship because though separated from my husband, I still believe in 'What God hath joined together, let no man put asunder'," Evelyn quipped.

"But Bobby, I presume you've got no problem in your sexual orientation, right? You're not gay nor are you a misogynist," I kiddingly told him, my mischievous streak getting the better of me.

"Oh, no, Bobby is definitely straight but he won't jump

into somebody's underwear just like that," Evelyn reinforced Bobby's hearty laugh, and I followed suit.

Now, who would beg to disagree in the statement that "two people can be close without getting emotionally involved" and where platonic friendship could be more beautiful than that in the worldly level because of moral boundaries.

Postscript:

I brought her some fruit (the idea just came into my mind that morning) on that Sunday when I read her her write-up after the mass. While I was wheeling her back to her room, she confessed that early that morning, she prayed for somebody to bring her some fruit - which I did!

Was it mere coincidence or the fact that things just don't happen but they are caused? That's a S64 question for you.

Postscript to the postscript:

Evelyn died last August 2004 as a result of a fall from her bed, of which she never regained consciousness.

- STO. ROSARIO DEVOTION GROUP -

Every first Sunday of the month for eight years now, the regular choir members of "The Blue Acres" get a welcome reprieve from their usual 10:15 morning mass liturgy singing with that specific apostolate done with gusto by the Sto. Rosario Devotion Group, an all Filipino faith community.

With its entourage coming from different places in the Bay Area, the SRDG was the brainchild of Tony Ong who

migrated to the US in the early 80s. An unlikely break-
through for a successful Filipino businessman-turned-
convert from Buddhism to Catholicism was his decision to
propagate his devotion to our Lady of the Rosary.

With some friends sharing his same vision, Tony's group's
initial commitment was to bring the image of Our Lady of
the Rosary to a family every week in what is known as
the "block rosary," a traditional Marian practice. The Valley
View Way in South San Francisco was the starting point of
this apostolate. Furthermore, inspired by the Holy Spirit to
express a progressive attitude of prayer in action augmented
by the fact that most members have a God-given poten-
tial in music led them to form a choir who sings for spiritual upliftment upon invitation and on schedule, receiving
sincere accolade after each performance.

In 1994, Tony donated four more statues of the Blessed
Virgin Mary to four parishes in the Bay Area, the new
venues for the expansion of the "block rosary" apostolate: the Church of the Epiphany, St. Patrick Church, St.
Augustine Church, and the San Bruno Church. Likewise,
two Couples for Christ prayer groups in Sacramento and
Fremont were recipients of the fifth statue of our Lady. All
have efficient leaders who provide logistical dynamism to
assure well-coordinated mechanics within the context of
the group's objectives.

Every Sunday for six months in 1995, the SRDG was
under the tutelage of Noemi Castillo (former director of the
Office of Ethnic Ministries of the Archdiocese of San Francisco who retired last 2004) for their religious formation, a
must for their spiritual growth and eventually becoming a
faith community.

In the absence of Tony who went home to the Philippines for good, Tess Fernandez (a supervising nurse at St. Luke's Hospital in San Francisco) presently acts as the overall coordinator of the core group. With her are pianist Milo Duazo and his wife, Candy, serving as consultant; Pacita Yuson, the music coordinator; and Nieves Sanchez, the soloist. Unmindful of the gas hike, Tess' husband, Greg, provides transportation for SRDG's various commitments around the San Francisco Bay Area. Also providing enthusiastic support are: Frank and Rosey Carzon; Lily Churchill; Diony dela Cruz; Elvie dela Cruz; Gloria dela Cruz; Mellie Denzon; Jessica Foronda; Bert and Teresita Francisco; Sean Galino; Manny and Rosalie Rocamora; Jocelyn Sumalde and Raul Vidanes.

Under the guidance of Our Lady of the Rosary, the SRDG continues its ministries for God's greater glory.

- CONCLUSION -

If meeting all sorts of people and interacting with them on the personal level has been your bread and butter in your professional life, you would understand that a good sense of humor is a must to maintain your equilibrium.

Just like one time when seated near us at the choir, one elderly lady resident sneezed with all her might, of all time during the consecration of the host.

"Excuse me!" A fellow resident also in her wheelchair seated next to her thought it would be kind enough of her to offer the apology in her neighbor's behalf. She is the type who attends mass every Sunday with a rag doll that she proudly introduces to everyone she meets in the corridor as her baby, and we volunteers would play along with her.

"A-c-h-oo!" The protagonist did it again this time during the consecration of the water.

"Excuse me!" The same apology from the same "Emily Post".

Still, it was a Christian challenge not to be diverted by the latest bodily function beyond control.

"Excuse me yourself !" The protagonist made it clear this time she did not want anybody to remind her of her manners.

Boy, that was when pandemonium broke loose!

- XV -

Some Moral Lessons in the Soup Kitchen

The soup kitchen is located on the outskirts of the city in a sort of a warehouse maintained by the city government whose administration office is on the second floor. It is rather an organized structure complete on the first floor with restrooms, kitchen, and a formal mess hall. A short distance away are the railroad tracks of the Caltrain which toots its horn at an hourly interval with commuters from and to the Silicon Valley.

A congregation of priests who depends solely on donations for their various ministries believing in Divine Providence has been involved for twelve years now in serving dinner to the homeless (though not necessarily penniless) who line up in front of the building every afternoon at three, six days a week. Donated food is collected, prepared, and cooked in the morning by volunteers at the congregation's kitchen which is a good thirty-minute drive away. Then they are brought to the soup kitchen by a van where another group of volunteers wait and are versatile enough to provide logistical support: setting the tables for ten heads each, preparing on individual plates a well-balanced diet of vegetable salad, meat, bread, and dessert, and then distributing them after the gospel has been read and the grace before meals said.

"Oh, boy, how could a person eat all these," I asked the priest who was our team leader the very first Saturday that I helped them as I saw a great heap of food in each plate enough to satisfy one with a gargantuan appetite. A well-built volunteer was acting as marshall at the door so that the beneficiaries from heaven-knows-where of the day's blessings could get inside in single file with their baggage in tow and take their seats at the tables in an orderly manner. There was a hundred of them at that time, it being the middle of the month and their monthly general assistance checks which most had received from the city government the week before already gone for booze, drugs and what-have-you.

"Why, this is equivalent to my three meals, Father," I further emphasized.

"But of course! That's not a surprise considering that they eat only once a day and so far we have not had any lawsuit for their having suffered any stomach disorder from the food we had prepared for them " was his humorous repartee.

It made me want to ask him that $64 question of how could that be a possibility here in the US where there is a plethora of material wealth; of a similar scenario in front of a Walgreens pharmacy at Mission Street, where an African-American in tattered clothes with a can in hand would ask for a quarter for coffee while at the same time open the door for the customers going in and out of the store; or a Caucasian couple at Market Street displaying a placard in front of their comforter with a note, "Will Work for Food."

Necessity for the basic things in life sometimes kills off human pride in the same way that material superfluity sometimes breeds insatiability of the spirit and looks upon death as a great respite after finding that life is kaput with no more challenge. And this is clearly the enigmatic side of life. The first hypothesis shows that to be deprived of food, clothing, and shelter does not necessarily mean the end of the world but rather serves as a challenge to go on whatever the cost to the extent of sometimes sacrificing one's dignity or values; the second oftentimes immolates life, the greatest God-given gift to mankind when the human species discovers that such gift does not mean an iota to him anymore because of that nagging feeling of "I'm tired of living and want to end it all," the usual cry of despair of residents in nursing homes during their lucid moments when they are pondering how their relatives are just waiting for them to croak.

It was in the soup kitchen where my quest for spiritual enlightenment was made concrete. Just like the miracle of the bread and fishes, one would wonder about the endless amount of donated goods coming from Safeway stores and other well-known bakeries around the city and the fact that their donations are tax-deductible is moot and academic; those from the food banks or just some private persons who drop off the food and other needed items incognito. All these could always feed the undetermined number of people who come for dinner everyday aside from the leftovers that we take afterwards to a carehome or another nomadic group living under the flyover. Same goes with the food the good Fathers sometimes dole out on cold mornings to those undocumented migrant day laborers lining up a street near a big hospital in the city while waiting for an employer to pick them up to take them to his farm or any other work site where they would be paid $10 an hour "under-the-table" or tax-free for transient labor.

Not to mention the manpower to back up the religious staff in the visible form of volunteers who come from different faiths (Mormons, Baptists, Episcopalians, etc.) or in a spiritual limbo just like that atheist guy I met but motivated by a common desire to serve those who, he said, have less in life, more than enough proof to dispel any doubting Thomas of the belief in Divine Providence; how He always provides; how He invites different people in different ways to serve Him, and how He uses them regardless of who they are as instruments to do His will.

Or one time when I asked a co-volunteer of mine (who amazes me considering that he has never burned a finger while washing dishes twice a week for fifteen years now with hot water and without any gloves on) to help me pray for Albert (my youngest son in Manila, who had had a high fever for several days) and who, before we went home that afternoon, told me not to worry for he (Albert) was already okay. Upon reaching home, I immediately called up my husband who assured me that our son's fever had just subsided a while ago and all's well with him.

Or, my former plan of just helping once a month was changed because of that "itchy" sensation bugging me if I can't go to the soup kitchen once a week and the feeling that my day is complete afterwards.

Or, finding I enjoy more doing the menial job (which my aunt commented would make me a laughing stock if my friends in Manila saw me washing the dishes and mopping the floor, to which I answered, "I don't care a hoot!") for the homeless rather than go to weekly parties of my kith and kin, which bore me to death. At least, I could hit two birds with one stone doing the former – earning credits for the next life while at the same time keeping watch on my cholesterol level.

But it was also at the soup kitchen where I found out the dichotomy between doing what one wants to do and doing what one is supposed to do, a wistful desire to establish a relationship with a member of the opposite sex based purely on the platonic level devoid of emotional entanglement because of moral boundaries.

That was when I met and knew Mark, an Irish-American. He was one of my co-volunteers who had the same schedule as I although several years my senior in this ministry.

"Did you miss me?" That's what he said when he greeted me at the same time that he hugged me after failing to join us at the soup kitchen the week before.

"Oh, yes, we missed you washing the dishes with us last week," I emphasized the plural form "we" at the same time that I tried to disengage myself from his tight embrace which took me by surprise. Although I've been here in the US for a couple of years now where hugging and kissing are considered casual things, still I was not yet used to being the object of such a show of affection from a member of the opposite sex who is not related to me either by consanguinity or affinity. I still believed two people could be close without being familiar with each other. I'm sure he got the message right because after that incident, he never attempted any physical contact with me again.

Everything should have been okay with the status quo until I told him my day off at my job site would be changed from Saturday to Sunday and so would my schedule of helping at the soup kitchen.

"No, you should stick to the same schedule with me because we are soulmates!" He was adamant about it sounding as if I had no other choice and he had all the right to say so.

I decided to keep my cool because I did not want to make a scene at that time although deep within me, I was seething and wanted to give him a piece of my mind. Who does he think he is to impose his ideas on me when even my own father when he was still alive and my husband now who are for me the two most influential members of the male gender wouldn't dare do it, knowing I'd rather kowtow to a request than a command? Just like in the past, backing off is my best self-defense mechanism, specially when my sixth sense tells me I'm treading on hot grounds.

In hindsight, Mark and I have many things in common except for one thing: our status in life. He is single and a good man at that any girl worth her salt could consider herself lucky to have him; on the other hand, I am content-edly married to a wonderful guy (who may not be perfect but who is) with whom I have three equally wonderful kids (never mind if they have their harmless mischiefs sometimes showing they are just normal). Although this is America where almost everything under the sun is justifi-able from abortion to stem cell research, I am not yet liberated where a situation calls for endangering my being a true Christian wife and mother.

I am afraid we are the diminishing kind what with a lot of permissiveness around catering to the basest instinct.

- XVI -

Drawing the Golden Thread

"I pray to our Lord that when I've reached that stage where I'd be more of a burden than a blessing to those still living around me, He'd just take me away," my spiritual mom here in San Francisco would tell me when sometimes we'd talk about man's mortality and life after death.

"La vaquia e bruta", which means, "Growing old is no good". Mario, an Italian long-time resident at Sophie's carehome who died recently used to sigh when he could no longer attend the senior citizens' Friday social function because of total body weakness brought by age.

"If I can only walk to reach that place where I can totally rest, I'd do it," confessed my father to my sister a few months before he died.

"I'm so tired doing nothing that I don't care anymore!" I remembered Alice declaring to both of us during one of her depressed moments.

Which makes me deduce that there must be a stage in our life when we have reached the apogee, where "morir es descansar" or "to die is to rest" (last line of "Ultimo Adios" or "My Last Farewell" by Dr. Jose Rizal, our national hero in the Phil.). And in all possibilities, this is so regardless of whether you are 80 or 18; whatever is the texture or shade of your skin; whether you are in the have's or the have-not's; whether you are a "no read, no write" or have a string of degrees; a spiritual guru or an atheist; where your place of domicile is beside the point; or other yardstick for measuring being human with its frailties.

This must also be the reason or justification maintained by advocates of the physician-assisted suicide in their right-to-die stand. Likewise, the suicide bombers who firmly believe in sure martyrdom in blasting themselves to pieces cognizant of the collateral damage to the innocent around them. Or, those who jump at the Golden Gate Bridge or shot themselves to death because of bankruptcy in their business or feeling of self-inadequacy.

Yet at the other end of the line, such apex is not only a welcome respite for the protagonists but also those who stand to benefit from their demise, emotionally, financially, physically, and, believe it or not, even spiritually.

Just like in 1995 when I was training for the first time for my job at a carehome somewhere in South San Francisco, we had a 90-year old woman dying. When we called up her only son to tell him about his mom, he simply said, "Oh, it's all right. I'll just see her at the mortuary." One could shed tears not because of the thought of death but on how a son could be so callous to his mother dying all alone in her room in a carehome when he should have been there and he could be there if he wanted to to bid her adieu.

Or, when a daughter or son aspiring for her/his inheritance wishes her/his father long suffering from Parkinson's disease be gone from the face of the earth because he is just a "pain in the neck" - how much more if the poor parent depends on her/him for his basic needs? Having been exposed to volunteer work at The Blue Acres, it sometimes makes me think that most probably being institutionalized and subsidized by the government when you can no longer take care and support yourself is a much better scenario than staying with your flesh and blood who just look upon you as a nuisance and wish you're dead.

Or, when a developmentally disabled child long dumped in an institution and now a possible candidate for the "next picture" could let his parents heave a sigh of relief saying, "good riddance" to a piece of an unwanted baggage.

Or, when one says a prayer of thanks for Martin Burnham and Edibora Yap, hostages in the Philippines, who at last were freed from their kidnappers after more than a year of captivity but everybody knew they died in the grace of the Lord.

As for me, I'll just "cross my bridge when I come to it."

An afterthought: I don't think the issue of death should be treated as a scary thing for it really will be our ultimate end. Rather, much thought should be given to how prepared we are to meet our Maker and give an accounting of what we did with what He gave us. Just like what Mother Teresa said:

"At the end of our lives, we will not be judged by how many diplomas we have received; how much money we have made or how many great things we have done. We will be judged by, 'I was hungry, and you gave me something to eat. I was naked, and you clothed me. I was homeless, and you took me in. I was in prison, and you visited me. I was sick, and you cared for me.'"

"Hungry, not only for bread – but hugry for love. Naked, not only for clothing – but naked of human dignity and respect. Homeless, not only for want of a room of bricks – but homeless because of rejection. "

"This is Christ in distressing disguise."

- XVII -

In Suspended Animation

Today is the 21st day of June, 2002, more than five years after I set foot on the US soil for the second time. "A lot of water has passed under the bridge", as the saying goes.

As I look out from the window of my room from the writing table left as junk and found for free (by my unidentified benefactor but which I considered godsend because I really needed one, a case where one man's garbage may be another's treasure just like in a garage sale) two weeks ago in front of the building beside ours, I could see clearly only a portion of the Golden Gate Bridge which on a foggy day is totally obscured from view. When I go out later today for my one-hour brisk walk which Dr. Romeo David (my primary care doctor who has that healing charisma to his patients just like Dr. Lawrence Wanetick, my breast surgeon) wants me to take everyday to lower my cholesterol and triglyceride levels, I will be able to admire the whole span of the bridge from a vantage point of view. Ditto with the rest of the beauty of creation.

Then, my eyes wander to the framed picture of my

family taken in 1996 at the gardens of San Agustin Church in Manila, the venue of grand weddings and equally pompous receptions afterwards. That was the big day of my brother-in-law's younger brother, Joel Lustria, who is a lawyer when he married Grace Perez, a school physician.

Thank God, we are still intact as a family. Rudy, my dear husband, aside from running his small business in Quiapo, Manila, has proven himself to be the pillar of strength (at a closer context than I) to our kids in their needs: *physical* (all three are pleasantly plump from the food he prepares personally for them with occasional coaching from me via long distance calls two or three times a week) and clean (he sometimes does the laundry in the absence of our laundry-woman, the only domestic chore my father didn't know how to do when he was still alive); *emotional* (he sometimes complains to me how our kids drive him bananas by their endless "Daddy, where are my briefs?" "Daddy, how about my shoes?" Daddy this, Daddy that so that I retort laughingly, "Oh, well, you should be flattered because your kids still look upon you as a demigod and can't do anything without you." To which he'd say, "No, thanks," although he admits that deep in his heart there are only the four of us with his kids who matter most to him; *spiritual* (though more of a pragmatist than I and deep in his ministry as a eucharistic minister in Manila for twenty years now, he checks that the "Sunday is a Family Day" tradition, my parents' legacy to all of us, is still observed with his kids in my absence: Sunday mass then go out for lunch afterwards).

Arnold, my eldest at 22, will be completing his studies in computer science at Adamson University also in Manila (where I taught English and had fond memories of my Engineering and Mass Com students) hopefully next year. The theories he learns in school he will apply hands-on to his small computer shop I had invested in for him which is right next to his dad's eatery.

MC, 21, after graduation from the college of nursing of the University of Santo Tomas (the oldest university in the Far East), reviewed and had just passed the board exams (our latest blessing) and is now a registered nurse in the Philippines. She told me she is not attracted to the opportunities the nursing profession offers worldwide but still plans to pursue her childhood dream of becoming a doctor ("I want to help a lot people." That's what she used to answer when, as a kid, asked why she wanted to be a pediatrician) to which I advised her to pray for guidance - if God wants her to serve Him as a doctor and if it is for His greater glory, He will surely help her to be one. Admitting that she is not yet burned out academically, she is now enrolled in subjects she had not taken up in the nursing curriculum but which are required for admission to the college of medicine in addition to passing its entrance examination slated in December for which she is also reviewing every Sunday.

Albert (who will be 18 come October 14), that smart aleck youngest son of ours (who one time confided to me he wanted to be a priest which must have stemmed from his parish work exposures), has just graduated from the high school department of San Beda College, an exclusive school for boys run by the Benedictines where he was a consistent deportment awardee. He also won first place in the poetry reading contest of their school during his senior year. He is now a freshman at La Salle – St. Benilde, taking up Information Management.

As for me, I still don't know where I'd be, what I will be, how I'd fare at this time next year, everything a $64 question - whether Alice and I will still be together, my dear client who, with her walker one Sunday afternoon, chased one of my relievers who was on duty at that time when the latter played exorcist and sprinkled her with holy water believing that her (Alice's) tantrum was the work of the devil; whether I'd still be here in San Francisco where I had encountered lessons 3 and 4 where men are concerned - that was a Sunday when dressed in a modest blouse and knee-length skirt for my assignment as lector at The Blue Acres and waiting for my bus, a truck stopped in front of me and the driver, a middle-aged white man, tried his best for five minutes to entice me to hop in but which I politely declined. No wonder there are women out there who are still missing after accepting rides from strangers ("Never trust a smiling dog"); or, that time when standing inside a jampacked Muni bus, I was shocked when I realized that this guy behind me was pushing maliciously his sort of sharp frontal accessory into my back that under ordinary circumstances, I could have jabbed my elbow against him but not wanting to create a scene, just eased my body in a subtle way to one side that getting my message, the jerk got off at the next bus stop, proving he still has a conscience after all.

But just like St. Augustine who had his epiphany regarding the Mystery of the Blessed Trinity from a child who actually was an angel, it took a complete stranger to be the instrument of mine.

That was when I met "Elizabeth," a lady who was also waiting for the same bus as I and confessed that she did not have any plan to be in our area that day, a week prior to my training for my new ministry, the eucharistic ministry to the homebound which I had finally decided to be committed to after two years of consideration. We enjoyed a rather interesting interaction and reached that point where I kiddingly shared that I told Somebody up there that if He really wants me to serve Him in this ministry, He better make me healthy, which He did because of negative results of my medical tests a few weeks ago. I further told her that if He really wants you to serve Him, just like a persistent lover, He won't take "no" for an answer and all the time, I've been playing hard to get.

"Oh, but He could have given those things to you without you making a deal with Him. He knows what you need and want even before you asking for them," she assured me amiably.

Later on, it dawned on me what beautiful food for thought that was. Could I discern a connection between the lines?

Just like in writing this memoir, He will decide whether or not I have ended my journey and guide me out of Uncle Sam's labyrinth into a certainty.

Postscript:

"I want to go home," Alice told me repeatedly when she was already in the last stage of her dementia. She can't even recognize her kids anymore.

In June 2003, she was brought to a care home where she died in her sleep two weeks after.

Epilogue

This book should have come out in June 2004 but did
not materialize because my first publisher declared bankruptcy in December 2003. He had been in the publishing
business for thirty-one years. However, believing that things
don't just happen but that they are caused, the hiatus was
more of a " blessing in disguise" because it allowed me to
view many variables in a much clearer perspective. It also
strengthened my faith and conviction on how one could be
a living testimony of braving all human odds to prove that if
God wants it done, He's going to provide the means.

Humility dictates that one should not boast his own
good deeds. On the contrary, I simply think that sometimes altruistic involvements deserve exposure if they're
worthy of commendation. So much so that this being the
last chapter of *Featherstitch*, it is more than my pleasure to
feature two groups of "warm bodies" showing they could be
"the light of the world", the "salt of the earth".

"The Good Shepherd Prayer Group"

Formed in 1993 under the umbrella of "The Light of God Community" at the Saint Elizabeth's Parish on Holyoke Street in San Francisco, Ca., it is a conglomeration of other Filipino parishioners in the San Francisco Bay Area. Their common spiritual bond? Being generous enough in still serving the Lord despite their day-to-day struggle to pursue the American Dream.

The Corpus Christi church on Santa Rosa Ave. in San Francisco is the venue of their music ministry every first Wednesday of the month, where they give more meaning to the marian devotees' novena to the Perpetual Succor. Other beneficiaries are the residents at the Laguna Honda Hospital, a hospice for the elderly poor and disabled, and those ladies in the sunset of their lives at the University Mound also in San Francisco.

They could also shed off their professional identities by being humble enough to serve the homeless at the soup kitchen of the Missionaries of Charity, the congregation of nuns founded by Mother Teresa of Calcutta, in the same way that they could be counted to show empathy and support for somebody whose loved one has "gone home to the Lord".

Bible study after saying the rosary is scheduled every Wednesday for introspection and discernment as to being instruments of the Lord – a continuing renewal of their faith after having undergone a seminar prior to their acceptance to the group.

The group has, likewise, reached out overseas by undertaking a vocation ministry in the Philippines for six years now. To date, they are benefactors to fourteen seminarians finishing their theological formation. Not to mention their positive response to requests for donations in the land of their birth. They also sponsor a nursing student in India who is now in her sophomore year.

Maintaining the balance of that call of both the spirit and the flesh, you could see them enjoying the lighter side of life in family camping trips, ballroom dancing where many members are adroit in the latest dance steps, picnics and interacting socially with other church groups like the Knights of Columbus and Barkada ni Jesus.

"The burden is light when done for the love of our Lord," says Tessie Garcia Alano, the present leader of the group who, in her own quiet ways, has her own personal ministries. Her husband, Adolfo, Sr., a successful architect who heads "Alano's Architectural Services", is her "partner in sanctity".

Other co-laborers in this particular vineyard are Stanley and Gloria Austria, Luz Diaz, Annie Gandeza, Tessie Gotangco, Jun Madriaga, Rolly Mungues, Regina Nebre, Marlene Parizal, Beth Pasco, Julia Pasco, Edward Rivera, Danny and Maria Salvador, Charles Sebastian, Rupert and Lourdes Ubaldo, Arthur and Alice Valiente, and Toney and Ethel Valiente.

"The University of San Agustin Alumni Association
– Northern California –

And Their Concept of Giving Back"

"Four years ago I felt very lucky for being chosen as a USAAA-NC scholar. The screening was not easy for I had to undergo examination and interviews. But eventually, I made it. Now I am a fully-fledged graduate, finishing with academic distinction. I am so grateful that you have been there for four long years with your support," thus wrote Rena Jardiolin from the University of San Agustin, Iloilo City, Philippines.

She could have been in that milieu where college education is an elusive dream because of financial constraints, the usual scenario in the Philippines. But, she was given a break which would enable her to "fish for life" and hopefully make a dent in her life.

And for Purple Tayo, a multi-awarded student leader at Archbishop Mitty High School in San Jose, Ca., the $500 grant from the Association in 2002 helped her when she started college, aside from the recognition she got as their local scholar.

Zenaida Yuson, as the first president of USAAA-NC, spearheaded this landmark vision. She was a member of the Philippine Bar Association prior to her migration to the United States.

The quarterly meetings, as provided for in their constitution and by-laws, were both for fellowship and brainstorming sessions, culminated by "passing the hat around" for a

$1 collection from all those present earmarked for "Asilo de Molo", an orphanage in Iloilo City run by the Dominican sisters. This is presently still an ongoing project.

In 1992, an alumni scholarship program was launched for the benefit of the members' children in the Northern California chapter. Mae Lourdes Quiapo Combong (AB English, Class of 1970) professionally worked out the mechanics as chairman which eventually led to the recipients also at the group's alma mater in Iloilo City.

It was at this time that the $10,000 proceeds from the raffle and beauty contest conducted by Siony Palacios (BSE, Class of 1959) as president helped build the four-story Alumni Building at the school campus.

Tom Calvo proved to be an effective leader from 1993 to 1994.

The Association's name is one of those etched at the entrance of the San Francisco main library in recognition of their $1000 donation, kudos to Linda Eugenio (BS Commerce, Class of 1962) in 1995. She likewise bolstered camaraderie and physical fitness among the Augustinians around by sponsoring basketball tournaments.

Dione Nemenzo (BS Pharmacy, Class of 1956) continued the Association's commendable undertakings in 1997 through 1998.

Yonie del Rosario (AB Economics, Class of 1980), who was consistently on the Dean's List in college and an active fundraiser of the group, followed suit in 1999-2000. And so with Art Asuncion (BS Architecture, Class of 1980) who took over as president from 2001 to 2002.

The president during 2003 to 2004, Allen Capalla (BS Chemistry, Class of 1982) exuded her dynamism when she headed the group last July 2004. It was on a homecoming centennial celebration of their alma mater where the 100 Outstanding Augustinians of the Century were honored. Dennis Jereza, Rose Herico and Siony Palacios, the Association's nominees were chosen in the community service category. It was also at this time that they handed in their 200,000 PHP donation to Reverend Father Manuel Vergara, OSA, present President of the University to help defray the cost of the school's various projects. Father Vergara subsequently ackowledged and thanked the Association for their generous gift. Likewise, the Association also gave 10,000 PHP to the "Asilo de Molo".

Elected just last January 2005, Ed Durias (Commerce, Class of 1971) is a successful real estate agent for five years now with Century 21 Su Casa. His project proposals include to reinvigorate the rather lethargic flow of the group's membership and to further raise funds, the life-blood of any organizational set-up.

Other Augustinians in the San Francisco Bay Area who have also lived the relevance of their Augustinian education deserve to be mentioned:

- Attorney Ismael Firmalino, Jr. (AB English Cum Laude, Class of 1972; Law Cum Laude Class of 1976) is a successful personal injury lawyer in San Jose, Ca.

- Ed Combong (AB English, Class of 1969) is the music coordinator handling seven choirs at the Parish of St. Joseph in Pinole, Ca.

- Rose Herico (BS Pharmacy, Class of 1957) is the Founder/ Elder of the Immaculate Conception Prayer Community in San Francisco, Ca. Aside from spiritual blessings in her life, she also has received many awards in her homecare and hospice services from several private and state associations here in California.

Earning one's laurels in the academe is undisputedly an accomplishment. However, what will make it more meaningful is when we give it back with commitment, compassion and hope. By then we could say, in our own small way, we did something to make this world a better place to live in.

Handumanan
(Lyrics by Ed Combong)

Ang handumanan
Nga yari sa akon dughan
Pagtulon-an nga gin pangabudlayan
Bulotho-an
Nga naghatag kinaalam
Kadungganan kag pangabuhi-an

Chorus:
Salamat sa mahal nga Ginoo
San Agustin gintukod mo
Salamat sa mahal nga Ginoo
San Agustin gintukod mo

Kasan-o lamang
Ang handum ko natuman
Nagbunga na ang gintinguha-an
Ang kaayo mo
Nag-iwag sang buas damlag ko
San Agustin gikan tanan sa imo

Salamat sa mahal nga Ginoo
San Agustin gintukod mo
Salamat sa mahal nga Ginoo
San Agustin gintukod mo

Alma Mater nga gugma ko
San Agustin, San Agustin
San Agustin, San Agustin

About the Author

Meriam Baniel Dela Cruz comes from Barotac Nuevo, Iloilo; finished Bachelor of Arts major in English – Political Science with special units in Journalism, Magna Cum Laude, from the University of San Agustin in Iloilo City; was staff assistant at the Government Service Insurance System (GSIS) – Manila for sixteen years; English Professor at Colegio San Agustin – Bacolod, Iloilo Maritime Academy & Adamson University; had some of her short stories and poems published in national magazines - all these in Philippines setting.

Since 1999 up to the present, she has been doing volunteer work at the Pastoral Care Department of the Laguna Honda Hospital, a hospice for the elderly poor and disabled in San Francisco, Ca. Sundays, you'll find her fulfilling her responsibilities as a chapel escort, choir member, lector & eucharistic minister to the homebound.

She had a one-year stint at the orphanage & home for the aged & dying of the Sisters of the Missionaries of Charity in Tayuman, Manila. That was a respite from her usual schedule at Mother Teresa's congregation's soup kitchen in San Francisco, Ca. where she helps feed the homeless of the city.

The first lady president of the Knights & Ladies of the Miraculous Medal, a marian association at the St Vincent de Paul Parish Church, San Marcelino St., Ermita, Manila, Philippines, she has her prison ministry at the Western Police District also in Manila.

She has pledged a percentage of her royalties from *Featherstitch* to go to her charitable projects in the Philippines.